Identifying Waste on the Shopfloor

SHOPFLOOR SERIES

Identifying Waste on the Shopfloor

CREATED BY

The Productivity Press
Development Team

NEW YORK

Most Productivity Press books are available at quantity discounts when purchased in bulk. For more information contact our Customer Service Department (888-319-5852). Address all other inquires to:

Productivity Press
444 Park Avenue South, 7th floor
New York, NY 10016
United States of America
Telephone 212-686-5900
Fax: 212-686-5411
E-mail: info@productivitypress.com

Cover illustration by Gary Ragaglia
Content development by Diane Asay, LeanWisdom Communications and Publications, Portland Oregon
Page design and composition by William H. Brunson, Typography Services
Printed and bound by Malloy Lithographing, Inc. in the United States of America

Library of Congress Cataloging-in-Publication Data

Identifying waste on the shopfloor / created by the Productivity Press Development Team.
     p. cm. — (Shopfloor series)
  Includes bibliographical references.
   ISBN 1-56327-287-3 (pbk.)
   1. Production engineering.   2. Production management.   3. Production planning. 4. Production control. I. Productivity Development Team (Productivity Press) II. Series.
  TS176.I29   2003
  658.5—dc21

                          2003008104

12 11   10 9 8

Contents

Publisher's Message   ix

Getting Started   xi

The Purpose of This Book   xi
What This Book Is Based On   xi
Two Ways to Use This Book   xii
How to Get the Most Out of Your Reading   xii
An Overview of the Contents   xiv

Chapter 1. What Is Waste?   1

What Is Waste?   2
   Value-added   3
Why Does Waste Occur?   4
   Manufacturing   4
   Conveyance   4
   Inspection   4
   Equipment   4
   Control/management   5
How Does Waste Take Root?   5
The Classification of Waste   7
   The Three *MU*s   7
   The 5M + Q + S   7
   The Flow of Goods   8
   The Seven Deadly Wastes   10
The Benefits of Identifying and Eliminating Waste   12
   To the Company   12
   To Shopfloor Workers   12
In Conclusion   13
   Summary   13
   Reflections   14

Chapter 2. The Seven Deadly Wastes   15

Overproduction   16

    Causes of Overproduction   17

    How to Eliminate Overproduction   17

    Overproduction Checklist   17

Inventory   18

    Causes of Inventory   18

    How to Eliminate Inventory   20

    Inventory Checklist   20

Conveyance   21

    Causes of Conveyance   23

    How to Eliminate Conveyance   23

    Conveyance Checklist   24

Defects   24

    Causes of Defects   24

    How to Eliminate Defects   25

    Defects Checklist   26

Processing Waste   26

    Causes of Processing Waste   29

    How to Eliminate Processing Waste   29

    Processing Waste Checklist   29

Operation Waste   30

    Causes of Operation Waste   30

    How to Eliminate Operation Waste   30

    Operation Waste Checklist   31

Idle time   32

    Causes of Idle Time   32

    How to Eliminate Idle Time   33

    Idle Time Checklist   33

In Conclusion   34

    Summary   34

    Reflections   36

Chapter 3. How to Discover Waste   37

Using the Back Door   38
Bringing Latent Waste to the Surface   39
Analyzing Current Conditions   40
    The Arrow Diagram   40
    The Summary Chart of Flow Analysis   43
    The Operations Analysis Table   44
    The Standard Operations Combination Chart   45
    The Workshop Checklist for Major Waste Finding   47
In Conclusion   49
    Summary   49
    Reflections   50

Chapter 4. How to Remove Waste   51

Adopting the Necessary Attitude   52
Removing Waste in the Movement of Goods   53
    Retention and Conveyance   54
    Process Waiting   56
    Lot Waiting   57
Removing Waste in the Actions of People   60
    Adopt Seventeen Principles   61
Removing Waste in the Way People, Goods, and Machines
    Are Combined   62
In Conclusion   66
    Summary   66
    Reflections   68

Chapter 5. How to Prevent Waste   69

Standardization   70
Visual and Auditory Controls   71
     Red-tagging   71
     Signboards   71
     Outlining   72
     Andons   72
     Kanban   72
     Pitch and Inspection Buzzers   73
The 5W and 1H Sheet   73
     Five Key Concepts for Asking "Why" and "How"   75
Pointing to the Future   76
In Conclusion   77
     Summary   77
     Reflections   78

Chapter 6. Reflections and Conclusions   79

An Implementation Summary   80
Reflecting on What You've Learned   82
Opportunities for Further Learning   82
Conclusions   82
Additional Resources Related to Identifying and
     Eliminating Waste   83
     The Shopfloor Series Books   83
     Other Books and Videos   85
     Newsletter   88
     Training and Consulting   88
     Website   88

About the Productivity Press Development Team   89

Publisher's Message

Identifying Waste on the Shopfloor combines all the topics of the Productivity Shopfloor Series into a single, fundamental focus— getting rid of waste. All lean production methods, using one strategy or another, have the primary intention of improving manufacturing methods to bring increased profits to the manufacturer and increased value and satisfaction to the customer. To increase profits and delight the customer, you have to get rid of waste—all those extraneous and counterproductive assumptions, attitudes, activities, materials, machines, operations, and processes.

In an organized and easy-to-assimilate manner, this compact book covers the "A" to "Z" of identifying and eliminating waste. It first shows you how to define waste and explains why it is such an insidious occurrence. It then describes different categories of waste and highlights the seven deadly wastes of manufacturing, listing causes and effective solutions. For each of the seven types of waste, a checklist is provided to help you examine your own workplace and prioritize your improvement efforts. Next, tools are provided to help you discover hard-to-find waste. Important guidelines and principles for removing waste are then discussed. And finally, practices that effectively prevent waste from creeping back into your workplace are described.

Like our other shopfloor books, this book is brought to you in an instructional design format to make the learning efficient and enjoyable. In the "Getting Started" section, strategies for effective learning are presented. Throughout each chapter, margin assists highlight key terms, key points, examples, and new tools. There are questions that help you apply the learning to your own workplace, and there are illustrations and cartoons to reinforce the learning. Each chapter has a summary for quick review.

If you can appreciate the value of conceptualizing and structuring your factory improvement efforts with the focus of eliminating waste, and would like a guide to help you apply all of the lean improvement methods toward that end, *Identifying Waste on the Shopfloor* is the book you need.

Acknowledgments

The development of *Identifying Waste on the Shopfloor* has been a team effort. Special thanks are due Diane Asay of LeanWisdom Communications and Publications for shaping the content. Michael Sinocchi provided project guidance. The cover illustration was provided by Gary Ragaglia of Metro Design. Mary Junewick coordinated the project tasks and did the copyediting. Guy Boster created the cartoons and illustrations. Typesetting and layout was done by Bill Brunson of Typography Services. Mike Ryder was our proofreader. And Bob Cooper managed the print process. Thanks also to Karen Gaines and Michael O'Neill of the marketing department for their promotional efforts.

We are very pleased to bring you this addition to our shopfloor series and wish you continued and increasing success on your lean journey.

Getting Started

The Purpose of This Book

Key Point

Identifying Waste on the Shopfloor was written to give you the information you need to participate in identifying and eliminating waste from your workplace. You are a valued member of your company's team; your knowledge, support, and participation are essential to the success of any major effort in your organization.

You may be reading this book because your team leader or manager asked you to do so. Or you may be reading it because you think it will provide information that will help you in your work. By the time you finish Chapter 1, you will have a better idea of how the information in this book can help you and your company eliminate waste and serve your customers more effectively.

What This Book Is Based On

BACKGROUND

This book is about an approach that is designed to eliminate waste from production processes. The methods and goals discussed here are closely related to the lean manufacturing system developed at Toyota Motor Company. Since 1979, Productivity, Inc. has brought information about these approaches to the United States through publications, events, training, and consulting. Today, top companies around the world are applying lean manufacturing principles to sustain their competitive edge.

Identifying Waste on the Shofloor draws from a wide variety of Productivity's resources. Its aim is to present the main concepts and steps of identifying and eliminating waste in a simple, illustrated format that is easy to read and understand.

Two Ways to Use This Book

There are at least two ways to use this book:

1. As the reading material for a learning group or study group process within your company.

2. For learning on your own.

Your company may decide to design its own learning group process based on *Identifying Waste on the Shopfloor*. Or, you may read this book for individual learning without formal group discussion. Either way, you will learn valuable concepts and techniques to apply to your daily work.

How to Get the Most Out of Your Reading

Becoming Familiar with This Book as a Whole

There are a few steps you can follow to make it easier to absorb the information in this book. Take as much time as you need to become familiar with the material. First, get a "big picture" view of the book by doing the following:

How-to Steps

1. Scan the Table of Contents to see how *Identifying Waste on the Shopfloor* is arranged.

2. Read the rest of this introductory section for an overview of the book's contents.

3. Flip through the book to get a feel for its style, flow, and design. Notice how the chapters are structured and glance at the illustrations.

Becoming Familiar with Each Chapter

After you have a sense of the structure of *Identifying Waste on the Shopfloor*, prepare to study one chapter at a time. For each chapter, we suggest you follow these steps to get the most out of your reading:

How-to Steps

1. Read the "Chapter Overview" to see what the chapter will cover.

2. Flip through the chapter, looking at the way it is laid out. Notice the bold headings and the key points flagged in the margins.

3. Now read the chapter. How long this takes depends on what you already know about the content and what you are trying to get out of your reading. Enhance your reading by doing the following:

- Use the margin assists to help you follow the flow of information.
- If the book is your own, use a highlighter to mark key information. You can make notes and answer questions in the margins. If the book is not your own, take notes on a separate piece of paper.
- Answer the "Take Five" questions in the text. These will help you absorb the information by reflecting on how you might apply it to your own workplace.

4. Read the "Summary" at the end of the chapter to reinforce what you have learned. If you read something in the summary that you don't remember, find that section in the chapter and review it.

5. Finally, read the "Reflections" questions at the end of the chapter. Think about these questions and write down your answers.

How a Reading Strategy Works

When reading a book, many people think they should start with the first word and read straight through until the end. This is not usually the best way to learn from a book. The steps that were just presented for how to read this book are a *strategy* for making your reading easier, more fun, and more effective.

Key Point

Reading strategy is based on two simple points about the way people learn. The first point is this: *It's difficult for your brain to absorb new information if it does not have a structure to place it in.* As an analogy, imagine trying to build a house without first putting up a framework.

Like building a frame for a house, you can give your brain a framework for the new information in the book by looking at the "Contents" and then flipping through the pages. Within each chapter, you repeat this process on a smaller scale by reading the "Chapter Overview" and then the key points, before reading the text.

Key Point

The second point about learning is this: *It is a lot easier to learn if you take in the information one layer at a time, instead of trying to absorb it all at once.* It's like finishing the walls of a house. First you lay down a coat of primer. When it's dry, you apply a coat of paint, and later a final finish coat.

Using the Margin Assists

As you've noticed by now, this book uses small images called *margin assists* to help you follow the information in each chapter. There are six types of margin assists:

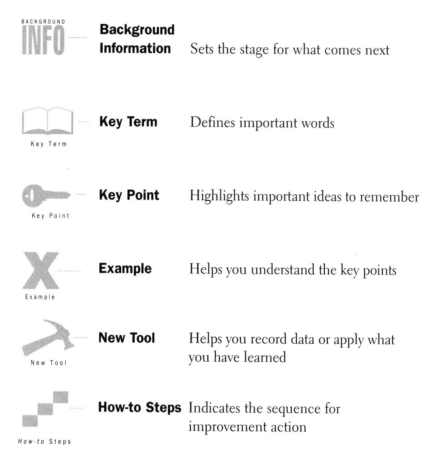

Background Information Sets the stage for what comes next

Key Term Defines important words

Key Point Highlights important ideas to remember

Example Helps you understand the key points

New Tool Helps you record data or apply what you have learned

How-to Steps Indicates the sequence for improvement action

An Overview of the Contents

Getting Started (pages xi–xv)

This is the section you have been reading. It has already explained the purpose of *Identifying Waste on the Shopfloor* and how it was written. Then it shared tips for getting the most out of your reading. Now, it will present a brief description of each chapter.

Chapter 1. What Is Waste? (pages 1–14)

Chapter 1 defines waste and value-added, and discusses the different categories of waste. It explores why waste occurs and how it gets rooted in standard processes, and shows the relationship between eliminating waste and creating lean production.

Chapter 2, The Seven Deadly Wastes (pages 15–36)

Chapter 2 defines and explores the seven deadly wastes. For each type of waste, causes are identified, methods are given to address the waste, and a checklist is provided to analyze the workplace and identify the waste.

Chapter 3: How to Discover Waste (pages 37–50)

Chapter 3 describes how to discover waste through the "back door" method, how to bring latent waste to the surface, and how to analyze current conditions using tools that focus on the flow of goods, people's actions, and the work combination of people, goods, and machines.

Chapter 4: How to Remove Waste (pages 51–68)

Chapter 4 describes the necessary attitude for removing waste, provides guidelines to help you remove waste, and describes the principles for removing waste from the movement of goods, people's actions, and the combination of worker and machine.

Chapter 5: How to Prevent Waste (pages 69–78)

Chapter 5 discusses tools and methods for preventing the further creation of waste and points to the advanced methods of lean production.

Chapter 6: Reflections and Conclusions (pages 79–88)

Chapter 6 presents reflections on and conclusions to this book. It includes a summary of the types of waste and how to discover, remove, and prevent waste. It also describes opportunities for further learning about techniques related to identifying and eliminating waste.

Chapter 1

What Is Waste?

CHAPTER OVERVIEW

What Is Waste?

    Value-added

Why Does Waste Occur?

    Manufacturing

    Conveyance

    Inspection

    Equipment

    Control/management

How Does Waste Take Root?

The Classification of Waste

    The Three *MU*s

    The 5M + Q + S

    The Flow of Goods

    The Seven Deadly Wastes

The Benefits of Identifying and Eliminating Waste

    To the Company

    To Shopfloor Workers

In Conclusion

    Summary

    Reflections

The Toyota Production System or *"just-in-time" manufacturing* is commonly defined as *the ability to make exactly what is needed, when it is needed, and in the amount it is needed*; in other words, the ability to respond to customer needs in every way. "Lean" production is the most recent name for this approach to production and gives a hint at how a "just-in-time" condition is achieved. Production flow must be created in order to respond to customer demand, and when production flow is attempted production waste comes to the surface. *Just-in-time* really means *the total elimination of waste*.

What Is Waste?

Each of us may have a different idea of what waste is, and it may change as conditions change. Sales people think inventory is wonderful when sales are up, but as soon as sales dip, inventory becomes a terrible burden. Telephones can be a source of waste, but not all telephone use is wasteful. Sometimes they are a necessary part of providing value for the customer, or for eliminating problems in flow to the customer. How can we all agree on a common definition of waste? Waste appears in great variety and often is mixed with non-waste. So let's look at what waste is *not* in order to gain a common understanding of what waste *is*.

Figure 1-1. Telephone Waste on the Shopfloor

Value-added

Key Term

Perhaps you have heard the word "value-added." In a factory, *value-added* means *those activities that change raw material into value for the customer.* Factory production serves the customer's need for a product. Value-added processes and operations are meant to directly serve the purpose of providing that product.

Example

For instance, in a screw-fastening operation we may ask, "What is the purpose of this operation? Is using a screw to fasten these two pieces together the most useful, the best way to hold them together?" If glue will work as well or better than a screw, perhaps the entire screw-fastening operation is waste. See Figure 1-2.

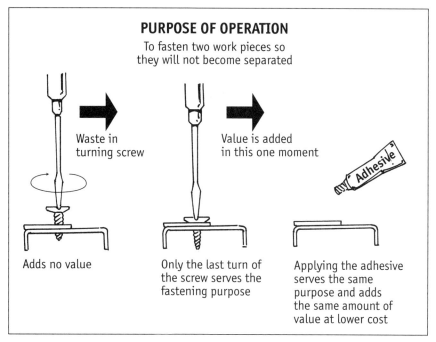

Figure 1-2. Waste in a Fastening Operation

When we see a pile of materials waiting to be processed we can ask, "Why is this material sitting here? Do we need this many? What is the lowest number of parts we need at this point to feed the downstream process?" By asking questions like this of every process and operation in the production flow we begin to get a handle on where the waste is. If a process or operation isn't adding value, question its purpose and seek ways to reduce or eliminate it.

Key Point

As we ask the purpose of each process and operation in this way we begin to identify what we mean by waste and what we mean by value-added. *The combination of processes and operations must be the best way to make that product, to deliver the highest quality, for the lowest cost, on time to the customer.*

Key Term

This leads us to an understanding of what we mean by waste. If what is not waste is all the things we do that are useful or value-added, then *waste is any activity that adds cost or time but does not add value.*

Why Does Waste Occur?

All kinds of problems occur in every factory, every shift, every day. How much waste a factory has depends on how well it responds to its problems. Let's look at possible responses to some different kinds of factory problems to get an idea about how waste occurs.

Manufacturing

- That guy is not busy now so I'll use him on this line for a little while.

- There's no place to put these things so let's put them down here for the time being.

Conveyance

- This stuff is heavy so let's borrow that forklift over there.

- Let's count these to make sure we have the amount we need.

Inspection

- We have been getting some complaints on quality so let's add some inspectors to this line.

- Some defects have been occurring in this process so let's increase output for a while to make sure we have enough good ones to fill the orders.

Equipment

- We need to increase our output so let's move in another machine for the time being.

- There's been some machine breakdown so let's call in the maintenance people for emergency repairs.

Control/management

- Next month's production schedule is not ready so let's repeat last month's.

- Let's make a list to keep track of all the late deliveries we seem to be getting.

What's wrong with these responses? On the surface they seem like common sense, but notice that they are all stopgap solutions. Not one asks why the problem is occurring. No response gets at the *cause* of the problem. It only solves it "for the time being" or addresses an "emergency." But these short-term solutions become standard operating procedures, don't they?

Key Point

This type of response to problems becomes the way of life in the factory unless someone starts to look deeper and solve the underlying causes that lead to these surface issues. *The heart of just-in-time or lean production is the willingness to look deeply into the issues that lie underneath any factory problem, and to solve problems by eliminating their causes.*

How Does Waste Take Root?

Example

There is a Thanksgiving story about a woman who every year cuts the turkey in half before putting it into the large roasting pan. One Thanksgiving one of her children asks her why she does this. She replies, "This is how my mother taught me to do it." So the child goes off to ask grandma why she cuts the turkey in half before roasting it, and grandma replies, "This is how my mother taught me to do it." As it happened, the child's great grandmother was still alive and was visiting for Thanksgiving also, so the child asks her the same question. Great grandmother thinks back to when she used to make Thanksgiving dinner and says, "Oh that was because I only had small pans in those days and the whole turkey didn't fit."

Key Point

This is how waste gets built into a process. We find solutions to conditions and then forget to change the solution when the conditions change. We no longer remember why we do certain things or what problem they were intended to solve. *It is important to ask why, over and over again, about everything we do. Only in this way will waste fail to take root.* See Figure 1-3.

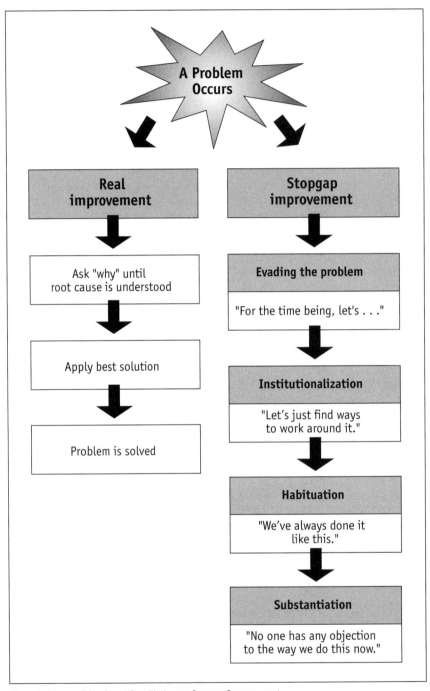

Figure 1-3. Waste Takes Root When We Accept Stopgap Improvement

The Classification of Waste

A number of methods for categorizing types of waste have emerged since lean production methods were developed. We will review some of these models to get a deeper understanding of what waste is and how to find it and eliminate it.

- The three *MUs*
- The 5M + Q + S
- The flow of goods
- The seven deadly wastes

The Three *MUs*

Key Point

In this way of thinking about waste *the goal is to achieve a condition where capacity and load are about equal.* In other words, there are just the right amount of workers and materials and machines to make just the right amount of product that is being ordered and deliver it on time to the customer. In Japanese this is expressed with the terms *muda, mura,* and *muri.*

- Muda (waste) = capacity exceeds load.
- Mura (inconsistency or variation) = capacity sometimes exceeds the load and the load sometimes exceeds capacity.
- Muri (irrationality) = load exceeds capacity.

By focusing improvement activities on eliminating the non-value-added activities throughout the production process, and on establishing production flow, a balance is naturally achieved between capacity and load.

The 5M + Q + S

Key Point

Another way of thinking about waste in a factory is to *focus on the areas where waste may occur:* the 5M (man, material, machine, method, and management), plus quality and safety. See Figure 1-4.

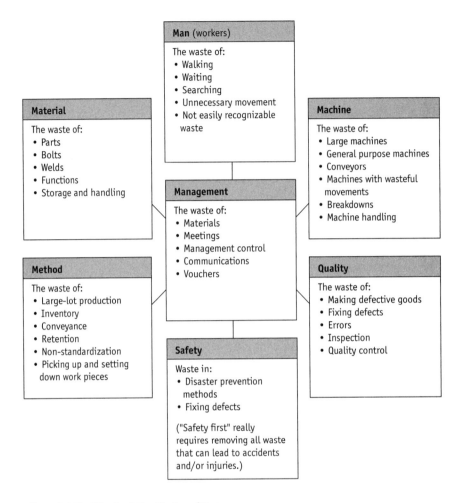

Figure 1-4. The 5M + Q + S Classification of Waste

Some of the main forms of waste that you will uncover by focusing on these aspects of production include, walking, waiting, searching, material storage and handling, large machines, conveyors, wasteful production methods, inventory, defective goods, errors, inspection, etc. All of these will be discussed throughout this book.

The Flow of Goods

Key Point

A third way of thinking about waste in a factory is to *focus on the flow of goods in production*. The flow of goods typically looks like this:

Materials are procured → Materials are *retained* in the warehouse → Materials are *conveyed* to processes on the production line → Materials are *retained* at the process equipment (WIP) → Materials are *picked up* for processing → **Materials are processed** → Processed goods are *set down* and *retained* on the other side of the processing machine (WIP) → Goods are *conveyed* to an inspection point → Goods are *retained until* inspected → Goods are *picked up* and *inspected* → Goods are *set down* and *retained* on the other side of the inspection process → Inspected goods are *conveyed* to the finished goods warehouse → Finished goods are *retained* prior to shipment → **Finished goods are delivered to the customer**.

Key Point

If you look carefully at this you will notice *there are really only four things going on: retention, conveyance, processing, and inspection.* Retention means stopping the flow of goods without adding any value to them. It is called stockpiling, warehousing, temporary storage, and so on. Retention produces inventory: materials inventory before processing, work-in-process inventory, or finished goods inventory. Inventory occurs for a variety of reasons:

- The upstream process moves faster than the downstream process.

- Goods flowing from several lines to one process or goods waiting to go from one process to several different lines tend to pile up.

- There is waiting for machine changeover.

- Materials are purchased and processed for expected end-of-the-month rushes.

- Materials are purchased in advance of orders.

- Spare parts are purchased in advance for after-sales service.

Key Term

Retention adds cost without adding value. It is easy to think that inventory solves production flow problems but in fact it just hides them. When you eliminate retention points the real problems in the production flow must be addressed directly. This is the only path to waste-free production flow, or lean production.

Key Term

Conveyance refers to *transporting goods without adding value.* Movement between retention points is often called "conveyance" and movement between a retention point and a process is often called "material handling."

Key Term

Processing means *adding value*. We either alter the raw materials or parts or we assemble parts to add value. Improvement of processes includes identifying how a process can best fulfill its purpose or identifying how a process can be done more efficiently. You will ask, Why are we drilling holes? Why are we putting in screws? You may discover many operations that can be replaced by better solutions or even eliminated.

Key Term

Inspection identifies and eliminates defects from the production flow. It does not add value because it does not eliminate the source of the defect but only its result. Once you change your focus from "finding" defects to "reducing" defects you are on your way to eliminating waste. Ultimately, lean production aims to prevent all defects from occurring.

TAKE FIVE

Take five minutes to think about these questions and to write down your answers:

1. Consider the four aspects of the flow of goods: retention, conveyance, processing, and inspection. How much of this is value-added? Can you think of ways to eliminate some of these steps?

2. Describe the flow of goods in your factory. How many retention points are there? How many types of conveyance are needed? Who inspects the goods and when?

The Seven Deadly Wastes

Key Points

The most well-known category of wastes is the "seven deadly wastes," which captures the essence of all the ideas discussed above and simplifies them to help you root out waste throughout your production process. You will need strongly motivated people with an instinct for seeing and removing waste. *Identifying and eliminating these seven types of waste will forge the path to lean production:*

- Overproduction

- Inventory

- Conveyance

- Defects
- Processing waste
- Operation waste
- Idle time

See Figure 1-5.

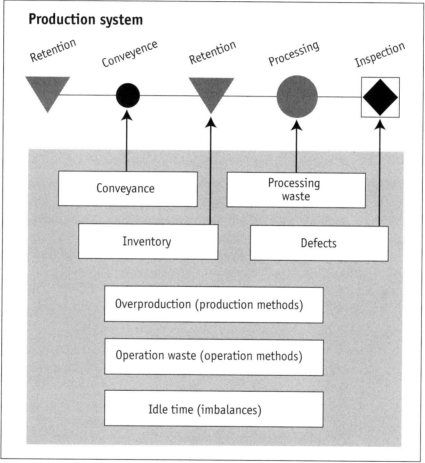

Figure 1-5. The Seven Deadly Wastes

How to identify these seven types of waste is discussed in detail in Chapter 2. The tools and attitudes needed to discover and remove waste are explored in Chapters 3 and 4, and the methods for preventing waste are discussed in Chapter 5.

The Benefits of Identifying and Eliminating Waste

Let's review some of the benefits of identifying and eliminating waste.

To the Company

Benefits to the company include:

1. *Cutting the hidden costs of production.* It is estimated that 80 percent of production activities and associated costs are non-value-added, or waste. When factories begin to focus on identifying and eliminating waste, the impact on the bottom line is astronomical.

2. *Increased customer satisfaction.* Customer satisfaction rises as a direct result of implementing lean production. When waste is eliminated from production, deliveries occur on time and product quality goes up.

To Shopfloor Workers

Benefits to individuals include:

1. *Increased job satisfaction.* No longer will you spend hours looking for missing tools, waiting for materials to arrive, walking around piles of inventory, lifting and setting down heavy parts or tools, working in unsafe conditions, and all the other things you have to do that aren't essential to your job. The frustrating non-value-added aspects of your job will disappear, and what you are trained to do and enjoy doing will be the major part of how you spend your time.

2. *Contributing to improvement.* Your ideas about how to improve your job will be listened to and you will participate in taking the frustration out of the workplace. Part of your job will be to find root causes and to create solutions that last. You won't have to make short-term fixes or live with someone else's short-term fix that no longer solves the problems you face.

There is no question that when production waste is rooted out everyone is happier. The flow of materials creates a hum in the workplace: a rhythm of the flow of materials from supplier to customer emerges as the value-added processes are freed up to operate at the rate of customer demand.

In Conclusion

SUMMARY

The Toyota Production System or *"just-in-time" manufacturing* is commonly defined as *the ability to make exactly what is needed, when it is needed, and in the amount it is needed*; in other words, the ability to respond to customer needs in every way. "Lean" production is the most recent name for this approach to production and gives a hint at how a "just-in-time" condition is achieved. *Just-in-time* really means *the total elimination of waste.*

In a factory, *value-added* means *those activities that change raw material into value for the customer. The combination of processes and operations must be the best way to make that product, to deliver the highest quality, for the lowest cost, on time to the customer.*

Waste is *any activity that adds cost or time but does not add value.* How much waste a factory has depends on how well it responds to its problems. *The heart of just-in-time or lean production is the willingness to look deeply into the issues that lie underneath any factory problem, and to solve problems by eliminating their causes.*

Waste gets built into a process because we find solutions to conditions and then forget to change the solution when the conditions change. *It is important to ask why, over and over again, about everything we do. Only in this way will waste fail to take root.*

Several methods for categorizing types of waste have emerged since lean production methods were developed. One way of thinking about waste is to *achieve a condition where capacity and load are about equal.* In other words, you focus on creating just the right amount of workers and materials and machines to make just the right amount of product that is being ordered and deliver it on time to the customer. When you eliminate production waste a balance is naturally achieved between capacity and load.

Another way of thinking about waste in a factory is to *focus on the areas where waste may occur*: the 5M (man, material, machine, method, and management), plus quality and safety.

A third way of thinking about waste in a factory is to *focus on the flow of goods in production*. The flow of goods in most factories really includes only four things: retention, conveyance, processing, and inspection. *Retention adds cost without adding value. Conveyance* refers to *transporting goods without adding value. Processing* means *adding value*. We either alter the raw materials or parts or we assemble parts to add value. *Inspection identifies and eliminates defects from the production flow*. It does not add value because it does not eliminate the source of the defect but only its result.

The most well-known category of wastes is the "seven deadly wastes." Identifying and eliminating these seven types of waste will forge the path to lean production. They are overproduction, inventory, conveyance, defects, processing waste, operation waste, and idle time. This book will focus on how to identify these seven types of waste and eliminate them.

A company benefits from identifying and eliminating waste by cutting the hidden costs of production. It is estimated that 80 percent of production activities and associated costs are non-value-added or waste. In addition, customer satisfaction rises as a direct result of implementing lean production. Benefits to individuals include increased job satisfaction and the ability to contribute to the improvement of one's own job.

REFLECTIONS

Now that you have completed this chapter, take five minutes to think about these questions and to write down your answers:

- What did you learn from reading this chapter that stands out as particularly useful or interesting?

- Do you have any questions about the topics presented in this chapter? If so, what are they?

- What additional information do you need to fully understand the ideas presented in this chapter?

Chapter 2

The Seven Deadly Wastes

CHAPTER OVERVIEW

Overproduction
    Causes of Overproduction
    How to Eliminate Overproduction
    Overproduction Checklist

Inventory
    Causes of Inventory
    How to Eliminate Inventory
    Inventory Checklist

Conveyance
    Causes of Conveyance
    How to Eliminate Conveyance
    Conveyance Checklist

Defects
    Causes of Defects
    How to Eliminate Defects
    Defects Checklist

Processing Waste
    Causes of Processing Waste
    How to Eliminate Processing Waste
    Processing Waste Checklist

Operation Waste
    Causes of Operation Waste
    How to Eliminate Operation Waste
    Operation Waste Checklist

Idle Time
    Causes of Idle Time
    How to Eliminate Idle Time
    Idle Time Checklist

In Conclusion
    Summary
    Reflections

This chapter discusses each of the seven deadly wastes. For each type of waste that is defined, the causes and possible responses are listed. Examples are provided to give you ideas of what to look for and where to look, but there are thousands of examples that you will find that are unique to your own environment.

We have provided checklists to help you get started in analyzing your own workplace and identifying where these wastes exist. Add items to the checklists as you discover them, and train everyone to use the checklists to examine their own work.

For each method listed in the sections on how to eliminate the waste, there are shopfloor books that describe in detail how to implement the method and its associated tools. See pages 83 to 85 in Chapter 6 for a description of these books. In Chapter 6 you can also find other resources to help you use these tools and methods to remove production waste.

Overproduction

Key Term

Overproduction is the worst of the seven wastes; it is the exact opposite of just-in-time production. *Overproduction* means *making what is unnecessary, when it is unnecessary, and in unnecessary amounts*. It occurs when you manufacture items for which there are no orders.

Why would you choose to do this? Companies often have over-production as a result of large-lot manufacturing methods, or mass production. There are several unfortunate effects of overproduction:

- Anticipatory buying of parts and materials
- Blocked flow of goods
- Increased inventory
- No flexibility in planning
- Occurrence of defects

Causes of Overproduction

- Large-lot production

- Anticipatory production (producing product in advance of demand)

- Inability to achieve short changeover times with the large equipment used in mass production systems

- Creating enough stock to replace the number of defective parts produced

- Overstaffing, or too much equipment

- Machines that turn out parts too quickly

How to Eliminate Overproduction

In order to balance capacity and load without overproducing, you must implement the advanced methods of lean production:

- Full work

- Line balancing

- One-piece flow

- Pull production using kanban

- Quick-changeover operations

- Level production—small-lot, mixed production

Overproduction Checklist

New Tool

Use a checklist like the one in Figure 2-1 to analyze your operations and identify overproduction. Add any other items that are contributing to overproduction on your shopfloor.

As you use the lists throughout this chapter, give a magnitude rating to each item on the list. (See page 48 for a rating key.) Your totals will show you which of the seven categories of waste need attention first. As you find wastes, also make notes about causes or improvement ideas.

Overproduction Waste-finding Checklist				
Process:				Date:
Description of Waste	Yes	No	Magnitude	Causes and/or Improvement Plans
1. No production schedule or control boards.				
2. No leveling of production schedule.				
3. Production not in sync with production schedule.				
4. Items missing.				
5. Defective goods produced.				
6. Equipment breakdowns.				
7. Too much manual assistance required.				
8. Machines have too much capacity.				
9. Lots are grouped into batches.				
10. Using "push" production.				
11. Caravan style operations.				
12. Not balanced with next process.				
		Total		

Figure 2-1. Overproduction Waste-finding Checklist

Inventory

Key Term

Overproduction leads to increased inventory. See Figure 2-2. *Inventory* means any *goods that are being retained for any length of time, inside or outside the factory.* This includes raw materials, work-in-process, assembly parts, and finished goods.

In lean production, inventory is regarded as a symptom of a sick factory. Therefore, one of the best ways to begin finding waste is to look for retention points where inventory tends to pile up. Hiding behind the symptom of inventory piles you will find a variety of causes that need to be treated.

Causes of Inventory

- Acceptance of inventory as normal or as a "necessary evil"
- Poor equipment layout
- Long changeover times
- Shish-kabob or large-lot production

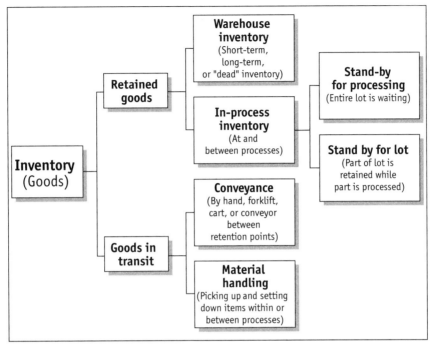

Figure 2-2. Types of Inventory

- Obstructed flow of goods (see Figure 2-3)

- Anticipatory production

- Defective parts

- Upstream process is too fast for the downstream process (see Figure 2-4)

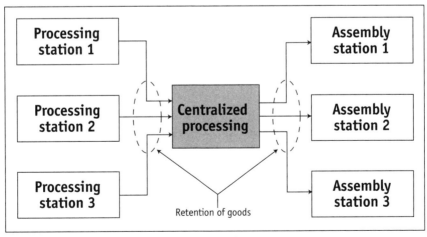

Figure 2-3. Accumulation of Inventory in the Flow of Goods

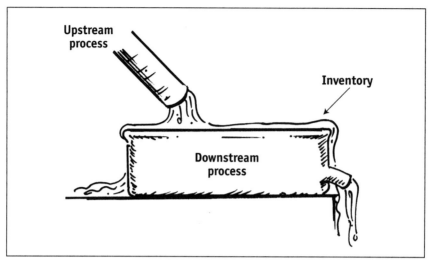

Figure 2-4. Unbalanced Production Line Inventory

Key Point

An "awareness revolution" must occur in everyone if inventory is to be eliminated. People must believe in the possibility of *zero inventory*. Inventory covers up problems; it never solves them. Only when everyone understands this will there be a commitment to analyze the causes of stockpiling and eliminate them.

How to Eliminate Inventory

- U-shaped manufacturing cells, layout of equipment by process instead of operation

- Production leveling

- Regulating the flow of production

- Pull production using kanban

- Quick changeover operations

Inventory Checklist

New Tool

Use a checklist like the one in Figure 2-5 to analyze your workplace and identify inventory. Add any other items relevant to inventory waste.

Inventory Waste-finding Checklist				
Process:				Date:
Description of Waste	Yes	No	Magni-tude	Causes and/or Improvement Plans
1. Lots of inventory on shelves and floors.				
2. Shelf and floor storage takes up lots of space.				
3. Inventory stacks block walkways.				
4. In-process inventory accumulates within individual operations.				
5. In-process inventory is stacked up between operators.				
6. In-process inventory is stacked up between processes.				
7. Impossible to visually determine quantities of in-process inventory.				
		Total		

Figure 2-5. Inventory Waste-finding Checklist

Conveyance

Key Term

More inventory naturally leads to more conveyance. *Conveyance* refers to *any transport or transference of materials, parts, assembly parts, or finished goods, from one place to another for any reason.* Material handling is one part of conveyance. See Figure 2-6 for an explanation of the difference between conveyance over a distance and material handling within a process.

Conveyance becomes necessary for a number of reasons:

- Poor layout
- Material handling—picking things up, setting things down, stacking things up
- Moving things around for any reason
- Excessive conveyance distances or heights
- Underutilization of systems that create flow

21

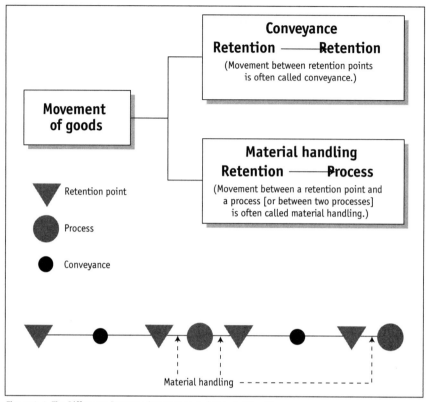

Figure 2-6. The Difference Between Conveyance and Material Handling

There are several ill effects of *conveyor systems.* They use up valuable space in the factory, increase conveyance-related worker hours, require more conveyance equipment, and often lead to damaged products. We do not expect to eliminate all transfer of goods within and between processes, but we can shorten conveyance distance and time and reduce or eliminate retention points. See Figure 2-7 for an explanation of material handling in one-piece flow production.

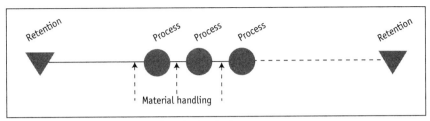

Figure 2-7. Material Handling in One-Piece Flow Production

Causes of Conveyance

- Poor layout

- Shish-kabob, large-lot production

- Single-skilled workers

- Sitting to perform operations

- The need for conveyance systems is assumed

How to Eliminate Conveyance

Basically, conveyance waste is corrected by redesigning equipment layout to create a flow between operations. Then you will be able to take out much of the complexity in the conveyance system and decrease material handling to a minimum. Some of the lean production methods that address conveyance follow:

- U-shaped manufacturing cells

- Flow production

- Multi-skilled workers

- Standing to perform operations

- Higher utilization rate

- Water beetles (material handlers in the kanban system of pull production)

Conveyance Checklist

New Tool

Use a checklist like the one in Figure 2-8 to analyze your operations and identify conveyance waste. Add items as needed.

Conveyance Waste-finding Checklist				
Process:				Date:
Description of Waste	Yes	No	Magni-tude	Causes and/or Improvement Plans
1. Pile up during conveyance.				
2. Change of conveyance devices in mid transfer.				
3. Previous and/or next process is on another floor.				
4. Conveyance requires manual assistance.				
5. Conveyance distance is too long.				
		Total		

Figure 2-8. Conveyance Waste-finding Checklist

Defects

Key Term

Defect waste includes *the defects themselves, the costs of inspecting for defects, responding to customer complaints, and making repairs,* all of which increase because of the defects themselves. Human errors create defects, as does variance in upper/lower tolerances in machine operations. When defects occur, customer complaints increase. This is one measure of defect rate. Stockpiles of defective products are another measure of this type of waste. When defects occur at a significant rate, inspection staff is often increased so that the defects are not passed on to the customer, and inventory may be increased to make up for the defective parts produced. In addition, productivity decreases and the cost of materials rises.

Causes of Defects

- Emphasis on downstream inspection
- No standards for inspection work
- Omission of standard operations
- Material handling and conveyance

How to Eliminate Defects

- Standard operations
- Mistake-proofing devices
- Full-lot inspection
- Building quality in at each process
- Flow production
- Elimination of the need to pick up and set down work pieces
- Improvement of jigs using human automation
- Promotion of value analysis and value engineering

Key Point

To reduce defects, their root cause must be found. Inspection that only sorts out the defective parts is not a solution to defect waste; it is actually one of the major defect-related wastes. Until you initiate back-to-the-source inspection and build quality into every process through standardization, the effects of defects will continue to disrupt the flow of goods and decrease productivity. Figure 2-9 shows that back-to-the-source inspection is the ultimate goal in lean production. It *prevents* defects at the source.

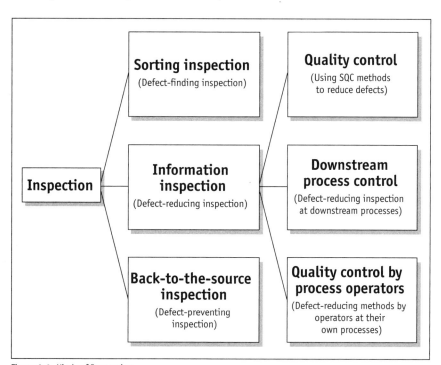

Figure 2-9. Kinds of Inspection

Defects Checklist

New Tool

Use a checklist like the one in Figure 2-10 to analyze your operations and identify defects. Add items as needed.

Defect Waste-finding Checklist				
Process:				Date:
Description of Waste	Yes	No	Magni-tude	Causes and/or Improvement Plans
1. Complaints from next process.				
2. Defects within the process.				
3. Human errors.				
4. Defects due to missing part(s).				
5. Defects due to wrong part(s).				
6. Omission(s) in processing.				
7. Defect(s) in processing.				
8. No human automation.				
9. No mistake-proofing.				
10. No inspection within process.				
11. Defects not addressed by improvement activities.				
		Total		

Figure 2-10. Defect Waste-finding Checklist

Processing Waste

Key Term

Processing waste refers to *operations and processes that may not be necessary*. An increase in defects may result from inappropriate or outdated operations or processes. Increased worker hours may result in process waste and defects. Lack of training or standardization may also produce process waste.

Design changes may eliminate the need for certain operations, yet workers may continue to do those operations because they don't yet understand the change. For instance, screw holes may continue to be drilled even though the fastening method has changed to welding or glue, or too many screws may be used. See Figure 2-11.

Figure 2-11. Lack of Processing Standards on the Shopfloor

Figures 2-12 and 2-13 show two examples of processing waste related to the operation of equipment.

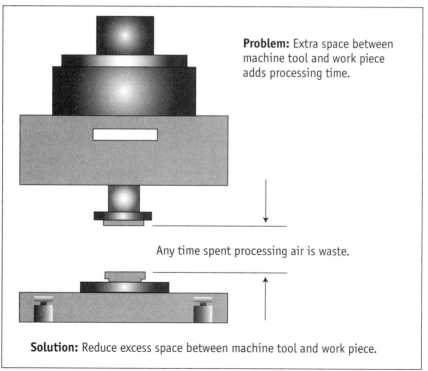

Problem: Extra space between machine tool and work piece adds processing time.

Any time spent processing air is waste.

Solution: Reduce excess space between machine tool and work piece.

Figure 2-12. Waste in a Machine Press

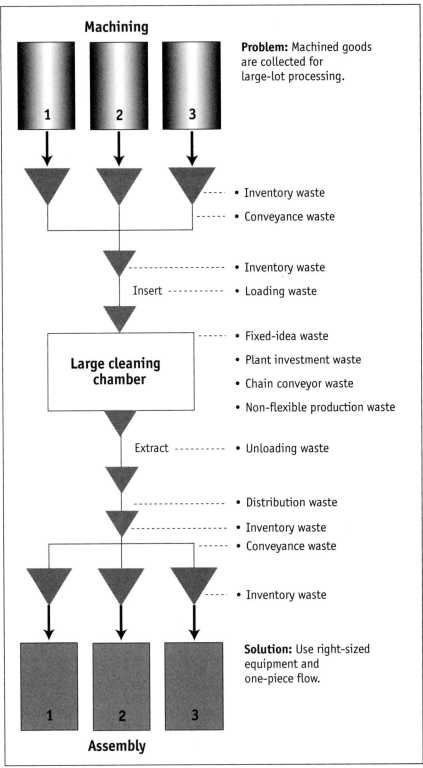

Figure 2-13. Waste Related to One Large Cleaning Chamber

Always ask, "What is the purpose of this particular operation?" And, "What is the function of this part?" Value engineering will help identify what is needed, and questioning why an operation is being done may lead to its elimination altogether.

Causes of Processing Waste

- Inadequate study of processes
- Inadequate study of operations
- Ill-suited jigs
- Incomplete standardization
- Materials are not studied

How to Eliminate Processing Waste

- More appropriate process design
- Review of operations
- Improvement of jigs using automation
- Thorough standardization
- Promotion of value analysis (VA) and value engineering (VE) techniques

Processing Waste Checklist

New Tool

Use a checklist like the one in Figure 2-14 to analyze your workplace and identify processing waste. Add items as needed.

Processing Waste-finding Checklist				
Process:				Date:
Description of Waste	Yes	No	Magni-tude	Causes and/or Improvement Plans
1. Process is not required for product function.				
2. Process includes unnecessary operations.				
3. Process can be replaced by something less wasteful.				
4. Part of process can be eliminated without detracting from product.				
	Total			

Figure 2-14. Processing Waste-finding Checklist

Operation Waste

Operation waste is similar to processing waste but relates more closely to the discrete movements of operators themselves. *Operation waste refers to movement that is not really needed to perform an operation.* Or it is to slow or too fast or too excessive or too awkward.

Key Term

Causes of Operation Waste

- Isolated operations
- Low employee morale
- Poor work layout
- Lack of training
- Undeveloped skills
- Instability in operations
- Increase in staff or worker hours

How to Eliminate Operation Waste

- Gradually switch to flow production
- Create U-shaped cell layout of equipment
- Make standardization thorough
- Increase training
- Increase operator awareness about motion during an operation

Key Term

Whereas many kinds of movement may be unnecessary, *work is the movement you do to add value to the product.* Movement that does not add value is waste. Find ways to reduce the amount of movement required to do your value-added work. Start by looking at the movement of your feet, then your hips, shoulders, arms, hands, and fingers.

Operation Waste Checklist

New Tool

Use a checklist like the one in Figure 2-15 to analyze your workplace and identify operation waste. If you notice any other kinds of operation waste, add them to the checklist.

Operation Waste-finding Checklist				
Process:				Date:
Description of Waste	**Yes**	**No**	**Magni-tude**	**Causes and/or Improvement Plans**
1. Walking.				
2. Turning around.				
3. Leaning sideways.				
4. Bending over.				
5. Too wide arm movements.				
6. Unnecessary wrist movements.				
7. Left or right hand is idle.				
8. Poorly utilized idle time.				
9. Wasteful work piece setup/removal.				
10. Non-standardized repetition of operations.				
11. Worker operates using different motions each time.				
12. Operations divided into too many little segments.				
		Total		

Figure 2-15. Operation Waste-finding Checklist

TAKE FIVE

Take five minutes to think about these questions and to write down your answers:

1. How much walking do you do in a day to perform value-added operations? (This does not mean when you go to lunch or take a break.) Wear a pedometer or use a stopwatch to measure the distance or time you spend walking while working.

2. How far do you have to reach to get a tool for the operation you perform? How many times do you have to pick up that tool in a day? Can you design your work area so that the tool is closer?

3. What other ways can you think of to eliminate motion while you do your work?

Idle time

Key Term

Idle time refers to both *human and machine waiting.* The need to wait may be caused by many things, including conveyance delays, machine failures, or some operators working too fast or too slow. It is important to examine the causes of idle time.

Causes of Idle Time

- Obstruction of flow

- Poor equipment layout

- Trouble at the upstream process

- Capacity imbalances

- Large-lot production

How to Eliminate Idle Time

- Production leveling
- Product-specific layout
- Mistake-proofing
- Human automation
- Quick changeover
- Autonomous maintenance
- Line balancing

Idle Time Checklist

New Tool

Use a checklist like the one in Figure 2-16 to analyze your work-place and identify idle time. If you notice any other reasons for idle time, add them to the checklist.

Idle Time Waste-finding Checklist				
Process:				**Date:**
Description of Waste	**Yes**	**No**	**Magni-tude**	**Causes and/or Improvement Plans**
1. Work piece delay from previous process.				
2. Machine busy status.				
3. Missing item(s).				
4. Lack of balance with previous process.				
5. Lack of planning.				
6. Lack of standard operations.				
7. Worker absence.				
8. Too many workers (more than two).				
		Total		

Figure 2-16. Idle Time Waste-finding Checklist

In Conclusion

SUMMARY

This chapter discusses the causes of each of the seven deadly wastes and provides checklists for analyzing your own workplace to identify where these wastes exist.

Overproduction is the worst of the seven wastes; it is the exact opposite of just-in-time production. *Overproduction* means *making what is unnecessary, when it is unnecessary, and in unnecessary amounts.* It occurs when you manufacture items for which there are no orders. Why would you choose to do this? Companies often have overproduction as a result of large-lot manufacturing methods, or mass production. In order to balance capacity and load without overproducing, you must implement the advanced methods of lean production.

Overproduction leads to increased inventory. *Inventory* means *any goods that are being retained for any length of time, inside or outside the factory.* This includes raw materials, work-in-process, assembly parts, and finished goods. In lean production, inventory is regarded as a symptom of a sick factory. Therefore, one of the best ways to begin finding waste is to look for retention points where inventory tends to pile up. Hiding behind the symptom of inventory piles you will find a variety of causes that need to be treated. *An "awareness revolution" must occur in everyone if inventory is to be eliminated.* People must believe in the possibility of *zero inventory.* Inventory covers up problems; it never solves them. Only when everyone understands this will there be a commitment to analyze the causes of stockpiling and eliminate them.

More inventory naturally leads to more conveyance. *Conveyance* refers to *any transport or transference of materials, parts, assembly parts, or finished goods, from one place to another for any reason.* There are several ill effects of *conveyor systems.* They use up valuable space in the factory, increase conveyance-related worker hours, require more conveyance equipment, and often lead to damaged products. Basically, conveyance waste is corrected by redesigning equipment layout to create a flow between operations. Then you will be able to take out much of the complexity in the conveyance system and decrease material handling to a minimum.

Defect waste includes *the defects themselves, the costs of inspecting for defects, responding to customer complaints, and making repairs*, all of which increase because of the defects themselves. Human errors create defects, as does variance in upper/lower tolerances in machine operations. When defects occur, customer complaints increase. This is one measure of defect rate. Stockpiles of defective products are another measure of this type of waste. When defects occur at a significant rate, inspection staff is often increased so that the defects are not passed on to the customer, and inventory may be increased to make up for the defective parts produced. In addition, productivity decreases and the cost of materials rises. *To reduce defects, their root cause must be found.* Inspection that only sorts out the defective parts is not a solution to defect waste; it is actually one of the major defect-related wastes. Until you initiate back-to-the-source inspection and build quality into every process through standardization, the effects of defects will continue to disrupt the flow of goods and decrease productivity.

Processing waste refers to *operations and processes that may not be necessary.* An increase in defects may result from inappropriate or outdated operations or processes. Increased worker hours may result in process waste and defects. Lack of training or standardization may also produce process waste. Always ask, "What is the purpose of this particular operation?" And, "What is the function of this part?" Value engineering will help identify what is needed, and questioning why an operation is being done may lead to its elimination altogether.

Operation-related waste is similar to processing waste but relates more closely to the discrete movements of operators themselves. *Operation waste* refers to *movement that is not really needed to perform an operation.* Or it is too slow or too fast or too excessive or too awkward. Whereas many kinds of movement may be unnecessary, *work* is *the movement you do to add value to the product.* Movement that does not add value is waste. Find ways to reduce the amount of movement required to do your value-added work. Start by looking at the movement of your feet, then your hips, shoulders, arms, hands, and fingers.

Idle time refers to both *human and machine waiting.* The need to wait may be caused by many things, including conveyance delays, machine failures, or some operators working too fast or too slow. It is important to examine the causes of idle time.

REFLECTIONS

Now that you have completed this chapter, take five minutes to think about these questions and to write down your answers:

- What did you learn from reading this chapter that stands out as particularly useful or interesting?

- Do you have any questions about the topics presented in this chapter? If so, what are they?

- What additional information do you need to fully understand the ideas presented in this chapter?

Chapter 3

How to Discover Waste

CHAPTER OVERVIEW

Using the Back Door

Bringing Latent Waste to the Surface

Analyzing Current Conditions

The Arrow Diagram

The Summary Chart of Flow Analysis

The Operations Analysis Table

The Standard Operations Combination Chart

The Workshop Checklist for Major Waste Finding

In Conclusion

Summary

Reflections

In this chapter we explore the tools for discovering waste. Once you have a theoretical understanding of the types of waste that occur in factory operations, as covered in the previous chapter, you must go straight to your factory floor and begin to look for waste everywhere.

Using the Back Door

It isn't easy to find waste when you look at the production line or the warehouse or an operation. If you have never been involved in improvement activities you will find it even harder to discover waste that may be right in front of you. It may take hours of just standing around watching people do what they do before you get a sense of where the waste is. Waste is everywhere, in every operation; it is so common and you are so used to it that it's hard to see. You may have to take the "back-door" approach and look for the opposite of waste: work.

Key Term

Work is the *value-added activity in the factory.* It is everything that waste is not. So when you can't see the waste, find the work. Everything else is waste!

You will need to closely inspect every operation in the entire process. Look at how machine screws are fastened. Ask why that operation is happening at that point. In the case of fastening two parts with a screw, the real work occurs only at that moment when the screw is tightened, the moment when the two pieces are fastened together. Picking up the screw, picking up the screwdriver, inserting the screw, turning the screwdriver until that last turn when the screw is tight—all are waste. Ask why the operator takes a step each time he turns the screwdriver. Ask why the box of screws is where it is. Could the operation be laid out better? Could the needed parts be closer?

Key Points

Continue to *ask "why" until you have explored the operation in depth* and are satisfied that you have uncovered the waste and understand the value of the operation or the need to eliminate it. *Ask "why" at least five times of every situation you examine.* This is part of the 5W and 1H approach that is discussed further in Chapter 5. This is one of the best ways to discover the waste embedded in operations. See Figure 3-1.

Discovering Waste Through the Back Door

1. **Look at the three *real* things:**
   The factory
   The facts
   Work-in-process

2. **Ask "What?"**
   Ask *what* the operation is about.

3. **Ask "Why?"**
   Ask *why* the operation is necessary.

4. **Everything that is not work is waste.**
   Once you have found out what the operation's essential function is, you can properly identify as waste everything in the operation that does not directly execute that function.

5. **Ask "Why?" at least five times to find root causes.**
   Ask *why* at least five times concerning each wasteful part of the operation. This will lead you to the real waste.

Draft an improvement plan.
Ask "How?"

Figure 3-1. Five Key Points for Discovering Waste Through the Back Door

---

TAKE FIVE

Take five minutes to think about these questions and to write down your answers:

1. Choose one operation in your line and identify the work being done. How much is left that is waste?

2. Consider an operation that you are responsible for and do the same thing.

Bringing Latent Waste to the Surface

If you are having difficulty finding waste, or there is no motivation to do so, you can jump-start the situation by introducing one-piece flow immediately. Don't wait for the right conditions, just put it in place with the current conditions in one line. Suddenly, latent waste will be obvious to everyone.

Example

You will notice that before one-piece flow, conveyors brought 50-unit loads, and now they must deliver 1 unit 50 times. Operators must walk all over the factory to go from one operation to the next because the machines are placed by function instead of process flow. You may discover that, even for operations that are close together, you have to carry the work piece by hand between them, where you used to use carts to shift a 50-unit lot a few feet. Also, giant cleaning chambers or drying ovens will seem vastly out of proportion when only one piece is moving through them, and so on. One-piece flow will also reveal the uselessness of stock shelves and poorly balanced processes in relation to the number of workers available.

Suddenly everyone will begin to grasp the nature of production waste and how to eliminate it.

Analyzing Current Conditions

There are several tools you can use to analyze current conditions quickly and effectively. We will describe five tools for discovering waste. Using Figures 3-3 through 3-7 as a guide, you can create your own 8-1/2- by-11-inch or larger templates of these forms for use on your shopfloor. The five tools are:

- The Arrow Diagram
- The Summary Chart of Flow Analysis
- The Operations Analysis Table
- The Standard Operations Combination Chart
- The Workshop Checklist for Major Waste Finding

The Arrow Diagram

New Tool

The *Arrow Diagram* focuses on the flow of goods to discover waste. (Arrow diagrams have recently been renamed value stream maps.) Many good books have been published on how to do value stream analysis using arrow diagrams. We include here a simple method for creating an arrow diagram to get a good understanding of your production process and to see where the waste exists in your factory.

The factors to be identified in your arrow diagram are retention, conveyance, processing, and inspection. There are specific symbols you use to indicate each of these aspects of a production process, as indicated in Figure 3-2.

Analysis factors	Symbols	Description	Amount of waste
Retention	▼	When the work-in-process flow is stopped (for other than conveyance, processing, or inspection)	Large
Conveyance	●	When the work-in-process is moved from one place to another	Large
Processing	●	When the work-in-process is changed physically or chemically for added value	There may be some waste in the process
Inspection	◆	When goods are inspected for conformance to quality and dimensional standards	Large

Figure 3-2. Process Analysis Symbols

There are four steps for creating your arrow diagram.

1. *Understand the purpose.* The purpose is to discover major forms of waste. The arrow diagram will help your improvement team "see" the waste.

2. *Select the product to be analyzed.* You can do a product/quantity (PQ) analysis to compare products and quantity. Choose products with a large output and those with many production problems as starting points for your analysis of current conditions using the arrow diagram.

3. *Prepare a factory layout diagram.* Include the entire factory layout, indicating the positions of machines, worktables, and other equipment. Store the original in a safe place so that you can make a copy of it each time you want to analyze another product line.

4. *Make the arrow diagram.* See Figure 3-3. Do this on the factory floor. Use the symbols in Figure 3-2 to show the different types of activities that occur. The map will help make the waste more obvious to you and your team than when you are simply standing on the factory floor observing standard operations. Connect the symbols with lines

that show the direction of the flow and the sequence of product through each operation. Create other symbols as you need to. At all conveyance points, note the conveyance distance and type of conveyance. At all retention points, note average work-in-process inventory.

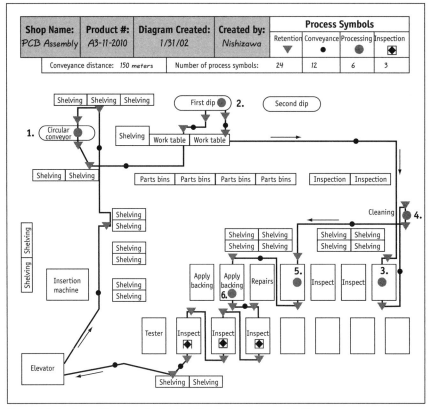

Figure 3-3. An Arrow Diagram of a Printed Circuit Board Assembly Shop

TAKE FIVE

Take five minutes to think about these questions and to write down your answers:

1. Is there a factory layout map you can copy to get started on your arrow diagram? Your supervisor or plant manager might have one. If not, then create one.

2. Using the symbols we have discussed, draw the process, retention, and inspection points in the line you are working on and connect them with conveyance routes. What are you learning about your work flow?

The Summary Chart of Flow Analysis

New Tool

Now that you have done an arrow diagram, write up a *Summary Chart of Flow Analysis*. See Figure 3-4. Count the symbols you used on the arrow diagram to show totals for the number of retention and conveyance and inspection points. Also note the total amount of goods retained and the total conveyance distance. Keep track of changes after improvements are made, using the same chart to compare.

		Before Improvement									After Improvement									
	Shop name **PCB Assembly**	Retention			Conveyance		Processing		Inspection		Retention			Conveyance		Processing		Inspection		
	Part name/number	# of times	# of units	Time	# of times	Distance	# of times	Lots	# of times	Lots	# of times	# of units	Time	# of times	Distance	# of times	Lots	# of times	Lots	
1	PCB1 (A3-11-2010)	24			12	150	6		3											

Date:

Figure 3-4. A Summary Chart of Flow Analysis

With these tools in hand, brainstorm improvement ideas. In brainstorming, you must let ideas flow freely. One unlikely suggestion may trigger a good idea. Select and further analyze good ideas.

The arrow diagram and the flow analysis should not take you too long or keep you away from your observation of the factory floor. Draw the arrow diagram while watching the production of the product on the floor and use it to help you see the waste there. Keep it relevant and keep looking. The whole purpose of using this tool and the others discussed in this chapter is to help you gain a "sixth sense" for waste. You *will* start to see the waste at some point as you do this, and when you do you will never be able to *not* see it again.

The Operations Analysis Table

New Tool

The *Operations Analysis Table* focuses on people's actions. As discussed in the previous chapters, not everything you do adds value. Operations analysis tables help you identify the waste in your own operations. See Figure 3-5. Either have your supervisor fill in the table or do it as a team, filling it in for each other. It's hard to do it for yourself because you can't watch yourself the same way someone else can. Eventually you will develop an awareness of your own motion and be able to identify, ever more precisely, when you are not adding value. But in the beginning, someone else must observe you and fill in the table.

Operations Analysis Table

Section: *Aluminum casting*   Operation: *Deburring*   Processes: *Press/drill*
Part number: *A11-21-301*   Author: *(name)*

Before Improvement		Date:			After Improvement		Date:		
Proc./Mat.Hdng./Conv./Idle/Insp.	Description of operation	Time	Distance		Proc./Mat.Hdng./Conv./Idle/Insp.	Description of operation	Time	Distance	
●○●▼⊞					●○●▼⊞				
●◐●▼⊞	Load castings onto cart	10'			◐○●▼⊞	Develop small shotblaster; install in U-cell			
●◐○▼⊞	Transfer to press	300			●○◐▼⊞	Transfer to press (via cart)		300	
●◐●▼⊞	Unload work pieces to be pressed	10'			◐○●▼⊞	Press			
●◐○▼⊞	Transfer to drill press	200			◐○●▼⊞	Drill			
●◐●▼⊞	Unload with work pieces to be drilled	10'			◐○●▼⊞	Shotblast			
◐○●▼⊞	Drill work pieces (lot size: 100 units)				●○●▼⊞	Inspect			
●◐●▼⊞	Load drilled work pieces onto cart	10'			●○●▼⊞				
●○◐▼⊞	Transfer to shotblaster	200			●○●▼⊞				
●○●◐⊞	Wait until shotblaster is empty	10'			●○●▼⊞				
●◐●▼⊞	Suspend work pieces in shotblaster w/crane				●○●▼⊞				
◐○●▼⊞	Shotblast work pieces (lot size—100 units)	3'			●○●▼⊞				
●◐○▼⊞	Load shotblasted work pieces onto cart	5'			●○●▼⊞				
●○◐▼⊞	Transfer to inspection station	500			●○●▼⊞				
●○●▼◐	Inspection (lot size: 100 units)	10'			●○●▼⊞				
●○●▼⊞					●○●▼⊞				
●○●▼⊞					●○●▼⊞				
●○●▼⊞					●○●▼⊞				
●○●▼⊞					●○●▼⊞				
●○●▼⊞					●○●▼⊞				
●○●▼⊞					●○●▼⊞				

Figure 3-5. Operations Analysis Table for an Aluminum Casting Deburring Operation

How-to Steps

1. *Fill in the table on the factory floor.* It is important to look at the real situation as you fill in the table, even if you know the situation by heart. As you fill in the form you will see things differently.

2. *Look for detail.* Write everything down that you possibly can.

3. Now *identify the waste.* Analyze as critically as you can to distinguish work from wasteful movement. Everything that is not value-added work must be counted as waste.

4. *Set an improvement goal.* Review all the data from your observation and decide what would be best to improve and how much improvement you expect.

5. *Eliminate waste.* Eliminate waste from everything except the real work operations. Write down the results of your improvement efforts on the "After Improvement" side of the table.

The Standard Operations Combination Chart

New Tool

Standard operations are a critical aspect of lean production. In order to create standard operations, current conditions must be understood and waste must be eliminated from all aspects of the process. A *Standard Operations Combination Chart* focuses on the relationship of people, goods, and machines. By plotting the cycle time of all activities in the process you can discover where the waste is and design the process to create a more efficient combination and reduce overall cycle time. See Figure 3-6 for an example of a combination chart. In the next chapter, Figure 4-10 shows one plant's use of a standard operations combination chart to record before and after improvements.

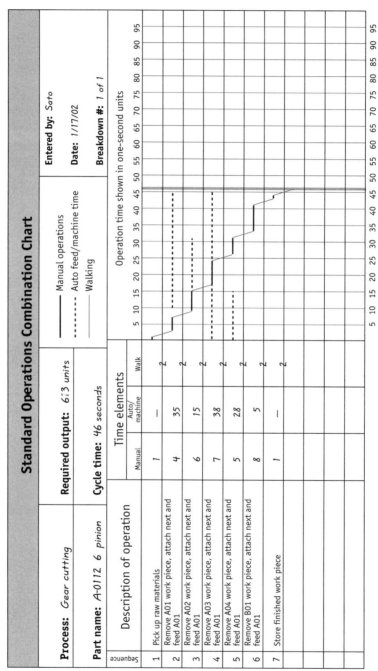

Figure 3-6. Standard Operations Combination Chart for a Gear Cutting Process

The Workshop Checklist for Major Waste Finding

New Tool

In the previous chapter we showed you detailed checklists for identifying specific instances of each one of the seven deadly wastes. The *Workshop Checklist for Major Waste Finding* allows you to identify—in a more general way—the seven types of waste in a work area. See Figure 3-7. You might want to use this checklist before using the detailed checklists. Checklists are good tools for identifying waste and recording improvement ideas.

Workshop Checklist for Major Waste Finding											
Workshop Name:										Date:	
#	Process Name	1 Overproduction waste	2 Inventory waste	3 Conveyance waste	4 Defect waste	5 Processing waste	6 Operation waste	7 Idle time waste	Waste Magnitude Total	Improvement Ranking	Improvement Ideas and Comments

Figure 3-7. Workshop Checklist for Major Waste Finding

How-to Steps

Use these four steps to follow to discover and remove waste.

1. Choose several processes or work areas and look for waste.

   a. Using Figure 3-7, find the *major* forms of waste at each process.

   b. Note the magnitude of each waste (see Figure 3-8).

2. Rank the improvements that are needed. Focus improvements on the process with the greatest total when you add up the magnitude columns.

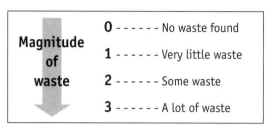

Magnitude of waste	**0** - - - - - - No waste found
	1 - - - - - - Very little waste
	2 - - - - - - Some waste
	3 - - - - - - A lot of waste

Figure 3-8. Four Levels of Magnitude

3. Choose the first process to be improved from the workshop checklist.

    a. Using the more *detailed* waste-finding checklists provided throughout Chapter 2, find more specific instances of waste.

    b. Observe the types and magnitude of the detailed waste.

4. Brainstorm improvement ideas and then carry them out.

TAKE FIVE

Take five minutes to think about these questions and to write down your answers:

1. Make a Workshop Checklist for Major Waste Finding and start filling it out for your work area. What interesting things do you discover?

2. What detailed waste-finding checklists would be useful in this area?

Figure 3-9. Do All Waste Analysis on the Shopfloor

In Conclusion

SUMMARY

In this chapter we explore the tools for discovering waste. It isn't easy to find waste when you look at the production line or the warehouse or an operation. It may take hours of just standing around watching people do what they do before you get a sense of where the waste is. Waste is everywhere, in every operation; it is so common and you are so used to it that it's hard to see. You may have to take the "back-door" approach and look for the opposite of waste: work.

Work is *the value-added activity in the factory.* It is everything that waste is not. So when you can't see the waste, find the work. Everything else is waste! You will need to closely inspect every operation in the entire process. *Ask "why" until you have explored the operation in depth. Ask "why" at least five times of every situation you examine.* This is part of the 5W and 1H approach that is discussed further in Chapter 5. This is one of the best ways to discover the waste embedded in operations.

If you are having difficulty finding waste, or there is no motiation to do so, then you can jump-start the situation by introducing one-piece flow immediately. Don't wait for the right conditions, just put it in place with the current conditions. Suddenly latent waste will rise to the surface and be obvious to everyone.

There are several tools you can use to analyze current conditions quickly and effectively. The *Arrow Diagram* focuses on the flow of goods to discover waste. (Arrow diagrams recently have been renamed value stream maps.) The *Summary Chart of Flow Analysis* helps you record and further analyze what you have found with the arrow diagram. The arrow diagram and flow analysis should not take you too long or keep you away from your observation of the factory floor. Draw the arrow diagram while watching the production of the product on the floor and use it to help you see the waste there. Keep it relevant and keep looking. The whole purpose of using this tool and the others discussed in this chapter is to help you gain a "sixth sense" for waste. You *will* start to see the waste at some point as you do this, and when you do you will never be able to *not* see it again.

The *Operations Analysis Table* focuses on people's actions. As discussed in the previous chapters, not everything you do adds value. Operations analysis tables help you identify the waste in your own operations. Either have your supervisor fill in the table or do it as a team, filling it in for each other. It's hard to do it for yourself because you can't watch yourself the same way someone else can. Eventually you will develop an awareness of your own motion and be able to identify, ever more precisely, when you are not adding value. But in the beginning, someone else must observe you and fill in the table.

Standard operations are a critical aspect of lean production. In order to create standard operations, current conditions must be understood and waste must be eliminated from all aspects of the process. A *Standard Operations Combination Chart* focuses on the relationship of people, goods, and machines. By plotting the cycle time of all activities in the process you can discover where the waste is and design the process to create a more efficient combination and reduce overall cycle time.

In the previous chapter we showed you detailed checklists for identifying specific instances of each of the seven deadly wastes. The *Workshop Checklist for Major Waste Finding* allows you to identify—in a more general way—the seven types of waste in a work area. You might want to use this checklist before using the detailed checklists. Checklists are good tools to identify waste and record improvement ideas.

REFLECTIONS

Now that you have completed this chapter, take five minutes to think about these questions and to write down your answers:

- What did you learn from reading this chapter that stands out as particularly useful or interesting?

- Do you have any questions about the topics presented in this chapter? If so, what are they?

- What additional information do you need to fully understand the ideas presented in this chapter?

Chapter 4

How to Remove Waste

CHAPTER OVERVIEW

Adopting the Necessary Attitude

Removing Waste in the Movement of Goods

Retention and Conveyance

Process Waiting

Lot Waiting

Removing Waste in the Actions of People

Adopt Seventeen Principles

Removing Waste in the Way People, Goods, and Machines Are Combined

In Conclusion

Summary

Reflections

We have defined waste, examined the causes of and some solutions to the seven deadly wastes, and looked at how to discover waste by using tools that analyze current conditions. In this chapter we describe some guidelines for removing waste.

Adopting the Necessary Attitude

First you must adopt an attitude that supports your ability to see waste. Waste is hard enough to find when you want to find it; if you don't want to find it, or if your response to finding it is denial or resistance, then it will never be possible for you to root out waste and make your work environment stress free.

Figure 4-1. Adopt a Waste-finding Attitude

Key Point

It's very important that you understand that *one purpose of discovering waste is to take the frustration out of your work.*

Many people will resist seeing the waste in their work. Just don't let it be you. You may hear yourself or others saying things like: "Let's not fix what ain't broke." "Can't we leave well enough alone?" "This is just another attempt to make us work harder for the same amount of money." "It looks good on paper, but it will never work on the floor." "We tried that twenty years ago. It didn't work then; it won't work now." "That's not my job." And so on.

You know the lines. You've probably said one or two of them at one time or another. We all have. Resistance is normal. Just don't let it keep you from learning to see the waste in your work. In the end, you are the one who suffers most from the results of waste.

Figure 4-2 lists some basic principles that will help you find waste and root it out. Learn them and practice them as often as you can. They help to create a "can do" attitude. *You may discover it can be fun to discover and eliminate waste in your job.*

Key Point

Ten Basic Principles for Improvement
1. Throw out all of your fixed ideas about how to do things.
2. Think of how the new method will work—not how it won't.
3. Don't accept excuses. Totally deny the status quo.
4. Don't seek perfection. A 50 percent implementation rate is fine as long as it's done on the spot.
5. Correct mistakes the moment they're found.
6. Don't spend a lot of money on improvements.
7. Problems give you a chance to use your brain.
8. Ask "Why?" at least five times until you find the ultimate cause.
9. Ten people's ideas are better than one person's.
10. Improvement knows no limits.

Figure 4-2. Ten Basic Principles for Improvement

Removing Waste in the Movement of Goods

We talked about making arrow diagrams to understand where the retention points in the process are and improving the conveyance routes or eliminating many of them with one-piece flow. Retention and conveyance are huge sources of waste.

Retention and Conveyance

But how do you remove the waste in the movement of goods once you have identified it? The best way to do it is to address the waste in this order:

1. Retention

2. Conveyance

3. Processing

4. Inspection

Following this order will ensure that you remove the major waste first. By the time you complete steps 1 and 2, more than half of the production waste will have been eliminated.

There is little or no movement of goods in processing and inspection; the focus here will be to create a layout so that retention and conveyance points can be eliminated more easily. Eventually, designated inspection points may drop out altogether as operators at every operation inspect their own work before passing it downstream.

Example

In the example shown in Figure 4-3, you see the before-and-after diagrams of the same factory we used in Chapter 3 to explain arrow diagrams. Before improvement, the factory occupied two floors; it had six major lines with 24 retention points, 12 conveyance points, and 3 inspection points.

First, we removed a number of retention and conveyance points and brought all the inspection points together in one place. In the "after" diagram there are still 14 retention points, 7 conveyance points, and 1 inspection point. There is much left to do, but now it is easier for everyone to experience the waste more easily and to work together on how to remove it.

The next improvement action that was taken at this factory was to remove all the points of retention in the process, which helped reduce the conveyance waste also. The next steps will include switching to one-piece flow and abolishing the lot system altogether. Next the factory will move to multi-process handling by each operator. This will require training and union support, and the equipment monuments will have to be dealt with somehow.

Before improvement

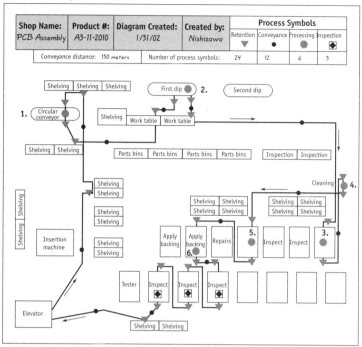

After first improvement

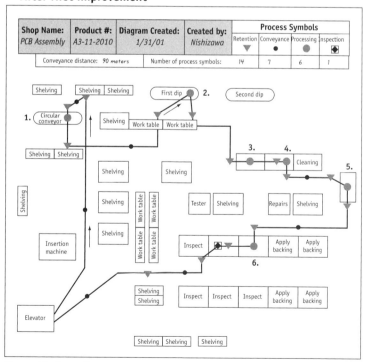

Figure 4-3. Arrow Diagrams of a Printed Circuit Board Assembly Shop —
Before and After Improvement

There are two types of retention that occur in production: process waiting and lot waiting. It is important to understand each of these and how to address them.

Process Waiting

Key Term

Process waiting means *the material or part is waiting its turn to be processed.* This occurs when the entire lot is kept waiting because of problems in the process itself. There are three reasons this may happen:

Capacity imbalances. Materials are ready for processing but must wait because the operator or machine is busy. This is caused either by capacity imbalance between processes, or when processed materials must be gathered at some processes and dispersed at others. Pull production keeps upstream processes from producing faster than downstream processes can handle. The goal is to synchronize processes so that material flows through them without any retention points.

Materials waiting. This occurs when an essential part is not on hand to start the processing. If the supplier is an outside vendor, then supplier relations must be addressed. If the source is within the factory, the cause may be machine failure, defects, or process imbalances of some kind. The cause must be investigated and eliminated.

Operation waiting. This means that the factory is understaffed and people are handling more than one station. First you must bring all operations into a single line and implement multi-process handling methods; then switch to one-piece flow.

TAKE FIVE

Take five minutes to think about these questions and to write down your answers:

1. What kind of process waiting occurs on your line?
2. How would you suggest reducing it? Can it be eliminated?

Lot Waiting

Key Term

Lot waiting means that *one part of the lot has been processed and the other part has not.* This is the nature of processing in lots instead of by one-piece-flow. There are four reasons lot processing is used.

Processes are separated. When this is the case, single-piece conveyance becomes impossible. To remove this form of waste you must change the layout of the equipment to minimize the distance between one step in the process and the next.

Mass production equipment is used. Equipment designed for high output often requires lot production or batch processing. The best solution is to right-size all your equipment, so that each process stays in sync with cycle time. But this may not always be an option. In that case you must design the flow around the monuments.

Changeover times are too long. Reducing setup times for all the machines in the line often eliminates the need for large lots. The aim is mixed-model production.

Operations are hard to balance. When skill levels of operators are uneven or there are labor-intensive operations within a line, it becomes difficult to establish wait-free flow. Line balancing will help this problem, and multiple-skill training will support multiprocess handling on the line so that operators can keep the flow going even in complex operations.

TAKE FIVE

Take five minutes to think about these questions and to write down your answers:

1. What kind of lot waiting occurs on your line?
2. How would you suggest reducing it? Can it be eliminated?

Figures 4-4 and 4-5 show a variety of ways to remove waste from both process waiting and lot waiting, as well as typical excuses that might be given by workers who don't yet have a "can do" attitude. Being forewarned of these excuses will help you counter them.

	Cause	Improvement Point (Waste Elimination)	Expected Resistance
Process Waiting	***Waiting for machines and/or people*** • **Unbalanced processes** Due to gap between previous and next process. 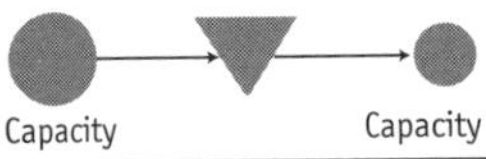 Capacity Capacity	• **Synchronization** Synchronize upstream process with downstream process. • **Pull production** Use a device or system (such as full work system) to keep the previous process from producing in excess of the next process's capacity.	• "This workshop is different. It's impossible here." • "The gap is due to different skill levels, so there's nothing we can do about it." • "So let's tell the previous process to let up a little."
	• **Accumulation/dispersion of processes** Work pieces for the same product are gathered at certain processes and spread out at others. 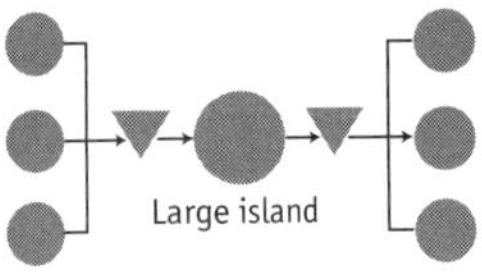 Large island	• **In-line layout (flow production)** Bring processes where work pieces accumulate apart from the rest of the line back into a closely linked line. • **Smaller equipment** Smaller machines that fit more easily into a closely linked line can be built inexpensively.	• "This machine is stuck here, so we can't have an in-line layout." • "I've never seen a small machine that can do this process." • "If we do that, we'll lose efficiency." • "They don't make machines like that." • "We'll have to spend a fortune buying new equipment!"
	Materials waiting • **Operations delayed by missing materials or parts** 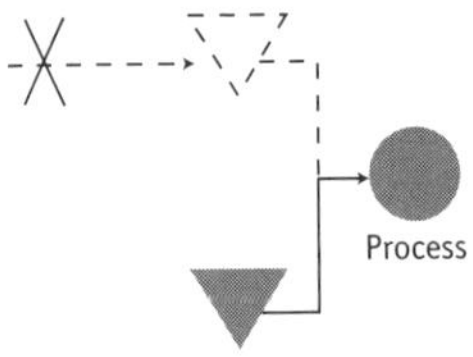 Process	***Parts from outside vendors*** • **Vendor guidance** Provide guidance and training in JIT and re-evaluate the vendor's delivery system. • **Reorganization** Reorganize based on number of orders and vendor evaluation. ***Parts from inside vendors*** • **The root cause** Address the root cause—defects, machine breakdowns, insufficient capacity, etc.	• "No, the vendor is a bigger company than we are." • "Sure, we can try to help them, but it won't do any good." • "It'll cost us more if we ask them to deliver more often." • "There's no way to avoid having those few defects." • "Machines break down because they're machines—it's inevitable."
	Operation waiting • **Caravan operations** The factory is understaffed and workers are processing lots at more than one process station. 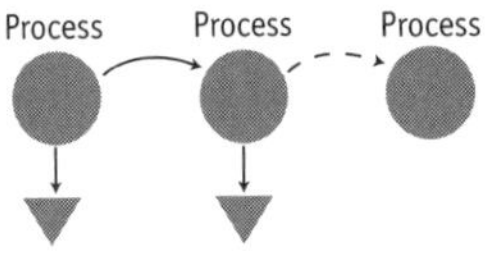 Process Process Process	• **In-line formation** Redesign the scattered processes into an in-line formation. • **Multi-process handling** Develop operations into multi-process handling. • **One-piece flow** Switch from shish-kabob production to one-piece flow.	• "We have no choice—we're short of workers right now." • "One-piece flow sounds like one big hassle. It wouldn't work."

Figure 4-4. Ways to Remove Waste in Process Waiting

	Cause	Improvement Point (Waste Elimination)	Expected Resistance
Lot Waiting	• **Processes are separated** 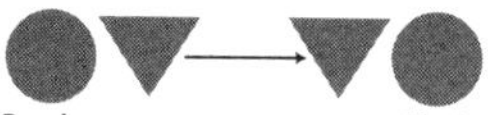 Previous Next	• **In-line** Line up the equipment according to the process sequence. • **One-piece flow** Switch to one-piece flow.	• "That machine can't be moved over here." • "That is a very high-precision machine, so it shouldn't be moved." • "One piece at a time? What are you talking about!?"
	• **Mass production equipment is used** Equipment is mainly designed for high output and cannot handle one-piece flow.  Mass production	• **Cycle time** Bring one-piece production in accordance with cycle time. • **One-piece production** Don't gather work pieces into batches for processing; always process just one at a time. • **Smaller equipment** Smaller machines that fit more easily into a closely linked line can be built inexpensively.	• "Making things one at a time has got to result in lower efficiency." • "I've never even heard of a machine built for one-piece processing." • "It'll get expensive if we start changing the equipment."
	• **Product changeover takes too much time**  Changeover	*Assembly* • **Changeover within cycle time** Changeover of parts, jigs, etc. should be able to be finished within the cycle time. • **Sequence feed or marshalling** Parts should be fed to the line according to the assembly sequence. *Processing* • **Changeover** Improve changeover to enable single changeovers or even zero changeovers.	• "There are just too many parts. It can't be done." • "If we do that, we'll need too much labor on the line." • "Changeover time can't be made any shorter than this."
	• **Operations are hard to balance** 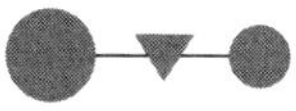	• **SOS system** Balance the line immediately and without further planning. • **Baton-passing method** Perform each operation at a prescribed pitch, then move directly on to the next one. • **Multi-process handling** Train workers to handle all processes on the line, from start to finish.	• "Stop the line? You must be crazy!" • "If we ever forget to pass the baton, there'll be lots of defects." • "Frankly, I don't think I could learn to handle so many processes."

Figure 4-5. Ways to Remove Waste in Lot Waiting

Removing Waste in the Actions of People

This type of waste includes all the motion in operator's bodies that occurs when they process materials: foot and hand motion, and torso movements such as bending, reaching, lifting, and so on. Foot movement may mean walking or it may simply mean the need to shift one's weight in order to reach for a tool. All of these things add waste, including operator fatigue. To remove waste, the action itself may need to be improved or the setup of the operation might need to be improved.

Key Point

This is your chance to examine what you do very carefully and find ways to eliminate unnecessary motion in your work. You may have been grumbling about how things are not set up properly for you to do your job with ease. Now is the time to do something about it. See Figure 4-6 for an example of how to analyze the operation you do and arrange your work area to minimize excess motion.

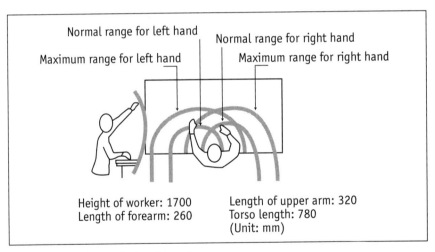

Figure 4-6. Range of Motion in Manual Operations

This focus on body motion is not just about reducing cycle time and establishing production flow, though these are very important results of such improvement activities. Most operators rejoice when they discover ways to eliminate the need to lift heavy dyes or overreach for tools and materials in order to do their jobs. Unnecessary motion such as continual twisting from your machine to a cart and back again can be eliminated and ease your work enormously.

Adopt Seventeen Principles

The rule of thumb for minimizing movement is to begin with the largest motions first—the arms, legs, and torso—and then gradually focus on smaller and smaller types of motion—hands, wrists, fingers, and head. Hiroyuki Hirano offers seventeen principles for identifying and reducing waste during operations.

Principles relating to the use of the body:

1. Start and stop manual operations using both hands in unison.

2. Keep arm motions simultaneous and symmetrical, the way you do when you are swimming—arms move in opposite directions with the same timing.

3. Minimize leg and torso motions. In assembly lines workers must often walk to the parts storage shelves and then back to the assembly area, or at the very least must twist to lift from a nearby cart or shelf, or reach up to a shelf above the work area.

4. Use gravity instead of muscle power.

5. Avoid motions that zigzag or turn sharply.

6. Make motions rhythmical. Find a rhythm for your work that is easy to maintain over time.

7. Ensure good posture and easy, fluid motions. Bending over to work on a low table or straining to work on a surface that is too high for you will make your work harder and lead to other types of waste.

8. Use the feet, too; for instance, to operate foot switches to lift parts or move materials to and away from you.

Principles relating to workplace layout:

9. Keep all necessary materials and tools close to you and in front of you.

10. Place materials and tools in their order of use. You can only do this if 5S is implemented and only a few parts are fed to your work area at a time.

11. Use inexpensive sources of power to feed materials through the operation.

12. Keep work tables and equipment at operator height.

13. Make the work environment comfortable.

Principles relating to jigs, tools, and machinery:

14. Let the feet work for switching operations, keeping the hands free.

15. Minimize tool variety by integrating tool functions wherever possible.

16. All materials and parts should be easy to pick up, below chest level, and containers should be within easy reach.

17. All handles and knobs should be in convenient locations and in easy-to-grasp shapes. All handles and switches should be within easy reach without moving the torso.

Removing Waste in the Way People, Goods, and Machines Are Combined

Remove anything that does not harmonize with production flow by designing the combination of people, materials, and machines so that they work in optimum relationship to each other. Standard operations combination charts like the one shown in the previous chapter (Figure 3-6) and at the end of this chapter (Figure 4-10) can help you do this.

Key Term

Let's look at three ways that people and machines can work together: serially, partially parallel, and in parallel. In a *serial operation* the *worker and machine take turns adding value to the materials*. See Figure 4-7.

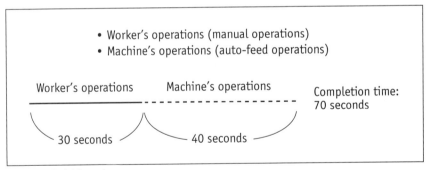

Figure 4-7. Serial Operations

Key Terms

In a *partially parallel operation* arrangement as shown in Figure 4-8, *worker activity and machine activity overlap*. In a *parallel operation, worker and machine work side by side at the same time*. See Figure 4-9.

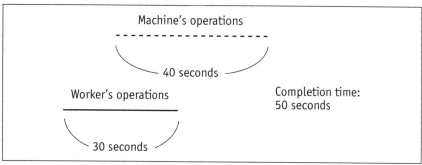

Figure 4-8. Partially Parallel Operations

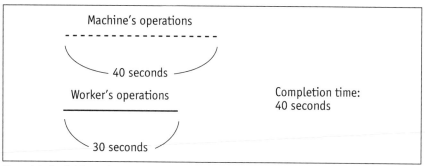

Figure 4-9. Parallel Operations

Key Points

In serial operations, aim to simplify the worker's share and mechanize the overall operation as much as possible. In parallel operations it helps to keep the worker separate from the machine. Brainstorm ways the machine can take over more of the worker's tasks, like pressing switches and other simple, easily mechanized aspects of an operation. In lean production, this is called *human automation.*

At this point you can begin to look at ways to separate the worker from materials by mechanizing the movement of single pieces through the operation. When you get to this point you are well on your way to removing waste from your factory. Figure 4-10 shows how to use standard operations combination charts to remove waste from production operations.

Before improvement

Standard Operations Combination Chart

Process no: 391-3637	No. required: 303 (600)	Entered by: *Kawano*
	Cycle time: *89" (54" needed)*	**Date:** 1/17/02
Item name: *Door jamb (lintel)*		**Analysis no:** 1 of 1

Sequence	Description of operation	Manual	Auto/machine	Walk
		Time elements		
1	Pull out work piece	3	—	2
2	Process S101 gain (small) at circular saw bench	15	10	2
3	Process S102 gain (large) at circular saw bench	23	18	2
4	Finish B101 hinge fastening at multi-spindle drilling	12	7	2
5	Insert edge (using cutter) at work table	13	—	2
6	Cut edge (using cutter) at work table	7	—	2
7	Set up new work piece	2	—	2

Manual operations
Auto feed/machine time
Walking

Operation time shown in one-second units

5 10 15 20 25 30 35 40 45 50 55 60 65 70 75 80 85 90 95

Why is the worker kept busy at the machine?

Why is the worker doing that and not the machine?

5 10 15 20 25 30 35 40 45 50 55 60 65 70 75 80 85 90 95

64

After first improvement

Standard Operations Combination Chart

Process no: 391-3637

No. required: 303 (600)

Cycle time: 53" (54" needed)

Item name: *Door jamb (lintel)*

Entered by: *Kawano*

Date: 1/31/02

Analysis no: 1 of 1

Operation time shown in one-second units

Sequence	Description of operation	Manual	Auto/machine	Walk
1	Pull out work piece	3	—	
2	Process S101 gain (small) at circular saw bench	5	10	2
3	Process S102 gain (large) at circular saw bench	5	18	2
4	Finish B101 hinge fastening at multi-spindle drilling	4	7	2
5	Insert edge (using cutter) at work table	13	—	2
6	Cut edge (using cutter) at work table	7	—	2
7	Set up new work piece	2	—	2

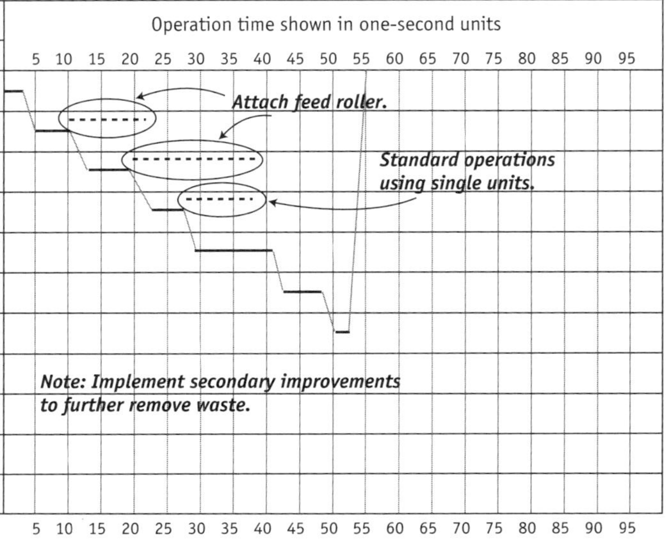

Legend: —— Manual operations; ------- Auto feed/machine time; ——— Walking

Attach feed roller.

Standard operations using single units.

Note: Implement secondary improvements to further remove waste.

Figure 4-10. Wood Product Manufacturer's Combination Charts — Before and After Improvement

In Conclusion

SUMMARY

In this chapter we describe some guidelines for removing waste. First you must adopt an attitude that supports your ability to see waste. Waste is hard enough to find when you want to find it; if you don't want to find it, or if your response to finding it is denial or resistance, then it will never be possible for you to root out waste and make your work environment stress free. It's very important that you understand that *one purpose of discovering waste is to take the frustration out of your work.* Resistance is normal. Just don't let it keep you from learning to see the waste in your work. In the end, you are the one who suffers most from the results of waste. If you adopt a "can do" attitude, *you may discover it can be fun to discover and eliminate waste in your job.*

How do you remove the waste in the movement of goods once you have identified it? The best way to do it is to address the waste in this order: retention, conveyance, processing, and inspection. Following this order will ensure that you remove the major waste first. By the time you complete steps 1 and 2, more than half of the production waste will have been eliminated. There is little or no movement of goods in processing and inspection; the focus here will be to create a layout so that retention and conveyance points can be eliminated more easily. Eventually, designated inspection points may drop out altogether as operators at every operation inspect their own work before passing it downstream.

There are two types of retention that occur in production: process waiting and lot waiting. It is important to understand each of these and how to address them. *Process waiting* means *the material or part is waiting its turn to be processed.* This occurs when the entire lot is kept waiting because of problems in the process itself. It can happen because of capacity imbalances, materials waiting, or operation waiting. *Lot waiting* means that *one part of the lot has been processed and the other part has not.* This is the nature of processing in lots instead of by one-piece-flow. It can happen because processes are separated, mass production equipment is used, changeover times are too long, or operations are hard to balance.

Removing waste in the actions of people refers to the motion of operator's bodies that occurs when they process materials: foot and hand motion, and torso movements such as bending, reaching, lifting, and so on. Foot movement may mean walking or it may simply mean the need to shift one's weight in order to reach for a tool. All of these things add waste, including operator fatigue. *This is your chance to examine what you do very carefully and find ways to eliminate unnecessary motion in your work.* You may have been grumbling about how things are not set up properly for you to do your job with ease. Now is the time to do something about it. The focus on body motion is not just about reducing cycle time and establishing production flow. Most operators rejoice when it becomes easier to do their jobs. The rule of thumb for minimizing movement is to begin with the largest motions first—the arms, legs, and torso—and then gradually focus on smaller and smaller types of motion—hands, wrists, fingers, and head.

To remove waste in the way people, goods, and machines are combined design the combination so that they work in optimum relationship to each other. Standard operations combination charts can help you do this. There are three ways that people and machines can work together: serially, partially parallel, and in parallel. In a *serial operation* the *worker and machine take turns adding value* to the materials. In a *partially parallel operation, worker activity and machine activity overlap.* In a *parallel operation, worker and machine work side by side at the same time. In serial operations, aim to simplify the worker's share and mechanize the overall operation as much as possible. In parallel operations it helps to keep the worker separate from the machine.* Brainstorm ways the machine can take over more of the worker's tasks, like pressing switches and other simple, easily mechanized aspects of an operation. In lean production, this is called *human automation.* At this point you can begin to look at ways to separate the worker from materials by mechanizing the movement of single pieces through the operation. Then you are well on your way to removing waste from your factory.

REFLECTIONS

Now that you have completed this chapter, take five minutes to think about these questions and to write down your answers:

• What did you learn from reading this chapter that stands out as particularly useful or interesting?

• Do you have any questions about the topics presented in this chapter? If so, what are they?

• What additional information do you need to fully understand the ideas presented in this chapter?

Chapter 5

How to Prevent Waste

CHAPTER OVERVIEW

Standardization

Visual and Auditory Controls

Red-tagging

Signboards

Outlining

Andons

Kanban

Pitch and Inspection Buzzers

The 5W and 1H Sheet

Five Key Concepts for Asking "Why" and "How"

Pointing to the Future

In Conclusion

Summary

Reflections

We have discussed how you discover waste and what to do to remove it; but it does not end there. Unfortunately, problems always crop up, and unless we *prevent* them from becoming sources of waste we will be right back where we started in no time at all. That is one reason why one of the very first things mentioned in this book about discovering waste was adopting the right attitude. If everyone is paying attention to keeping waste from taking hold, then you have a good chance of sustaining production flow. There are four important methods you can use for maintaining a waste-free production environment:

- Standardization

- Visual controls

- Auditory controls

- 5W and 1H

Standardization

Key Term

We mentioned standardization in Chapter 2 as an important way to remove waste, especially in preventing defects and processing waste. The primary purpose of standardization is to create and sustain a waste-free process. *Standardization* means *establishing standard procedures for every operation so that anyone can understand and use them—and everyone does.* There are many aspects to standardization. Standards must be created, documented, well-communicated, adhered to, and regularly re-assessed.

Standards are required for:

- Machines

- Operations

- Defining normal and abnormal conditions

- Clerical procedures

- Procurement

Visual and Auditory Controls

One way waste enters into operations is when standards are not improved to meet changing conditions. Even standardization fails to sustain waste-free production if not systematically updated to take advantage of new materials, new technology, and worker improvement ideas. If the slightest defect occurs, the standard must be reconsidered.

The factory is a living thing and must constantly be adjusted to stay responsive to changes in the environment. Responsiveness must be systematic so that problems are addressed without losing the solid foundation of the waste-removing methods already established. The best way to do this is through visual and auditory controls.

Red-tagging

You probably did this at the beginning of your improvement activities when you implemented 5S. If not, do it now: put a red tag on everything in the factory that is not necessary to the current operations of the production process. After everyone has had time to notice the red-tagged items and claim any that are needed in their area, remove the remaining red-tagged items from the environment. Management can decide what to do with them: they can be sold, thrown out, or moved to a location where they are needed. Always keep the production floor free of anything that is not directly part of the production process.

Signboards

The purpose of workstations and the names of the workers who operate them should be displayed at every processing point. Signboards can also identify equipment and processes so that everyone knows what things are and what they are used for. Standard quantities should be included on supply bins or carts. The products produced on each line or in each cell can be displayed, and so on.

Outlining

Borders around tools and equipment, big and small, help people find and return things. Outlining can also create patterns of work-flow by using the floor to indicate where and where not to place things, where to walk, safety zones, and danger zones. Outlining to indicate goods to be processed or parts that have been processed becomes a signal to material handlers for replenishing, or for delivery to the next process.

Andons

Different colored lights can report the status and needs of a system, and signal when defects or abnormal conditions occur so that problems can be solved immediately (Figure 5-1).

Figure 5-1. Visual Control on the Shopfloor

Kanban

These little signs accompany work-in-process. They are the flexible production instructions or work orders that trigger materials supply and production in a pull system, the hallmark of lean manufacturing.

Pitch and Inspection Buzzers

These indicate when operations get out of sync with demand or when defects are found. They keep awareness focused on solving problems and keep waste from taking root.

The 5W and 1H Sheet

New Tool

In Chapter 3 we mentioned asking "why" at least five times to discover waste and understand the root cause of problems. The 5W and 1H (five "whys" and one "how") is a powerful method and one that never stops being useful in sustaining a waste-free production environment. The *5W and 1H Sheet* is a tool that will help you systematically apply this method. Figure 5-2 shows one sheet filled out. (Use the side columns when multiple questions or answers arise at any step of solving a single problem.) Figure 5-3 shows an example of an improvement idea that resulted from the use of the 5W1H Sheet in Figure 5-2.

TAKE FIVE

Take five minutes to think about these questions and to write down your answers:

1. What kind of standardization exists in your workplace? How could it be improved?
2. What kinds of visual and auditory control are being used in your workplace? How could they be improved?
3. Apply the 5W and 1H Sheet to a problem on your line. What did you find out that you didn't know before?

5W and 1H Sheet

Problem:
The line stopped.

Why no. 1:	**Why no. 1:** Why did the line stop occur?	Why no. 1:

Current status:	**Current status:** The line stopped when a dimensional defect was found in a processed item.	Current status:
Why no. 2:	**Why no. 2:** Why did the dimensional defect occur?	Why no. 2:

Current status:	**Current status:** Two work pieces got processed at once.	Current status:
Why no. 3:	**Why no. 3:** Why did two work pieces get processed at once?	Why no. 3:

Current status:	**Current status:** The two work pieces got stuck together.	Current status:
Why no. 4:	**Why no. 4:** Why did two work pieces get stuck together?	Why no. 4:

Current status:	**Current status:** The wrong drill bit was used.	Current status:
Why no 5:	**Why no 5:** Why was the wrong drill bit used?	Why no 5:

Current status:	**Current status:** Drill bit storage is inadequate (drill bits are kept in a casual pile).	Current status:
Improvement proposal (How):	**Improvement proposal (How):** Devise storage improvement and reinforce the 5S.	**Improvement proposal (How):**

Figure 5-2. 5W and 1H Sheet

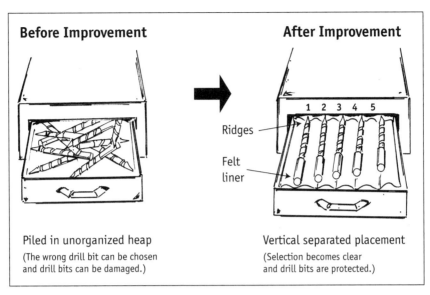

Figure 5-3. Improvement in Drill Bit Storage

Five Key Concepts for Asking "Why" and "How"

Follow these principles suggested by Hiroyuki Hirano when you are asking the 5 "whys" and 1 "how":

Look with the eyes of a child. All improvement begins with the first why. Never cease looking and never cease asking that first why. As you practice this, the rest will follow.

Remember three essentials for fact finding. (1) *Go* to where the problem occurred. (2) *See* the problem first-hand. (3) *Confirm* the facts based on your own observations.

Be a walker and an observer. Supervisors and managers must continually walk through the factory to see that standards are being followed and to practice seeing waste. Operators need to continually examine their own operations to stay alert for new problems and new ideas for solving them that may come to mind as they do their jobs (Figure 5-4).

Break down fixed thinking. If you ask "why" and "how" often enough you will eventually run out of "known" answers. At this point you may reach internal mental resistance to the discovery of what you don't know. Get in the habit of asking why and how beyond this point of fixed thinking. That is when you will make the big discoveries about waste and how to solve it.

Do it now. Don't wait. Put your ideas into practice immediately!

Figure 5-4. Maintain Constant Waste Patrol on the Shopfloor

Pointing to the Future

Advanced topics in waste identification and elimination are explored in the other books in this Shopfloor Series. They describe, in detail, the tools and methods of the Toyota Production System, or lean manufacturing. Descriptions of these books can be found on pages 83 to 85 of Chapter 6.

After reading this book and identifying the critical areas of significant waste in your factory, set up improvement teams, including the operators of the areas being addressed, and root it out. In addition, set up study sessions using the other books in the Shopfloor Series to address the solutions you choose to implement. Once the journey of seeing and removing waste is begun, the satisfying results will keep you improving without end.

In Conclusion

SUMMARY

We have discussed how you discover waste and what to do to remove it; but it does not end there. Unfortunately, problems always crop up, and unless we *prevent* them from becoming sources of waste we will be right back where we started in no time at all. There are four important methods you can use for maintaining a waste-free production environment: standardization, visual controls, auditory controls, and 5W and 1H.

The primary purpose of standardization is to create and sustain a waste-free process. *Standardization* means *establishing standard procedures for every operation so that anyone can understand and use them—and everyone does.* Standards must be created, documented, well-communicated, adhered to, and regularly re-assessed. One way waste enters into operations is when standards are not improved to meet changing conditions. Even standardization fails to sustain waste-free production if not systematically updated to take advantage of new materials, new technology, and worker improvement ideas. If the slightest defect occurs, the standard must be reconsidered. The factory is a living thing and must constantly be adjusted to stay responsive to changes in the environment. Responsiveness must be systematic so that problems are addressed without losing the solid foundation of the waste-removing methods already established. The best way to do this is through visual and auditory controls. Red-tagging, signboards, outlining, andons, kanban, and pitch and inspection buzzers are all tools you can use to stay alert to waste when it occurs.

We have discussed asking "why" at least five times in order discover waste and understand the root cause of problems. The 5W and 1H (five "whys" and one "how") is a powerful method and one that never stops being useful in sustaining a waste-free production environment. The *5W and 1H Sheet* is a tool that will help you systematically apply this method.

Follow these principles suggested by Hiroyuki Hirano when you are asking the 5 "whys" and 1 "how": Look with the eyes of a child, remember three essentials for fact finding; be a walker and an observer; break down fixed thinking; and do it now. Remember, always put your improvement ideas into practice immediately!

Advanced topics in waste identification and elimination are explored in the other books in this Shopfloor Series. They describe, in detail, the tools and methods of the Toyota Production System, or lean manufacturing. After reading this book and identifying the critical areas of significant waste in your factory, set up improvement teams, including the operators of the areas being addressed, and root it out. In addition, set up study sessions using the other books in the Shopfloor Series to address the solutions you choose to implement. Once the journey of seeing and removing waste is begun, the satisfying results will keep you improving without end.

REFLECTIONS

Now that you have completed this chapter, take five minutes to think about these questions and to write down your answers:

• What did you learn from reading this chapter that stands out as particularly useful or interesting?

• Do you have any questions about the topics presented in this chapter? If so, what are they?

• What additional information do you need to fully understand the ideas presented in this chapter?

Chapter 6

Reflections and Conclusions

CHAPTER OVERVIEW

An Implementation Summary

Reflecting on What You've Learned

Opportunities for Further Learning

Conclusions

Additional Resources Related to Identifying and Eliminating Waste

    The Shopfloor Series Books

    Other Books and Videos

    Newsletter

    Training and Consulting

    Website

An Implementation Summary

Identifying and Eliminating Waste on the Shopfloor

What Is Waste?

Waste is everything that is not value-added in producing product or service for the customer.

Types of Waste

1. According to the three *MUs* classification of waste, capacity, and load should be equal.

2. According to the 5M + Q + S classification of waste, improvement activities must focus on man, material, machine, method, management, quality, and safety.

3. According to the production flow classification of waste, which focuses on the flow of goods through a factory, four major types of waste exist: retention, conveyance, processing, and inspection.

4. According to lean production's primary classification of waste there are "seven deadly wastes."

The Seven Deadly Wastes

1. Overproduction

2. Inventory

3. Conveyance and material handling

4. Defects

5. Processing waste

6. Operation waste

7. Idle time

How to Discover Waste

1. Use the "back door" method. If you can't see waste, find the value-added work. Everything else is waste!

2. Bring latent waste to the surface by implementing one-piece flow in the current, unimproved conditions.

3. Analyze current conditions using arrow diagrams, summary charts of flow analysis, operations analysis tables, standard operations combination charts, and waste-finding checklists.

How to Remove Waste

1. Adopt an attitude that supports changing the way things have always been done.

2. Examine the four major sources of waste: retention, conveyance, processing, and inspection.

3. Improve the motion of people performing their jobs.

4. Eliminate unnecessary motion in machines.

5. Establish the optimum combination of people, machines, and materials.

How to Prevent Waste

1. Standardize.

2. Use visual and auditory controls.

3. Ask "why" five times, and then ask "how."

4. Keep improving your waste identification and elimination efforts.

Reflecting on What You've Learned

Key Point

An important part of learning is reflecting on what you've learned. Without this step, learning can't take place effectively. That's why we've asked you to reflect at the end of each chapter. And now that you've reached the end of the book, we'd like to ask you to reflect on what you've learned from the book as a whole.

Take ten minutes to think about the following questions and to write down your answers:

- What did you learn from reading this book that stands out as particularly useful or interesting?

- What ideas, concepts, and techniques have you learned that will be *most* useful to you as you learn to identify and eliminate waste? How will they be useful?

- What ideas, concepts, and techniques have you learned that will be *least* useful as you learn to identify and eliminate waste? Why won't they be useful?

- Do you have any questions about identifying and eliminating waste? If so, what are they?

Opportunities for Further Learning

How-to Steps

Here are some ways to learn more about identifying and eliminating production waste:

- Find other books, videos, or trainings on this subject. Several are listed on the next pages.

- If your company is already using methods to identify and eliminate waste, visit other departments or areas to see how they are applying the ideas and techniques you have learned about here.

- Find out how other companies have eliminated waste. You can do this by reading magazines and books about just-in-time or lean manufacturing, and by attending conferences and seminars presented by others.

Conclusions

Identifying and eliminating waste is more than a set of ideas or a series of techniques. It is a fundamental approach to improving the manufacturing process. We hope this book has given you a taste of how and why this approach can be helpful and effective for you in your work.

Additional Resources Related to Identifying and Eliminating Waste

The Shopfloor Series Books

Productivity Development Team, *Just-in-Time for Operators* (Productivity Press, 1998). This Shopfloor Series book is a concise and practical guide that will introduce equipment operators, assembly workers, and other frontline employees to the basic concepts, techniques, and benefits of JIT practices.

Productivity Press Development Team, *5S for Operators: Five Pillars of the Visual Workplace* (Productivity Press, 1996). This Shopfloor Series book outlines five key principles for creating a clean, visually organized workplace that is easy and safe to work in. Contains numerous tools, illustrated examples, and how-to steps, as well as discussion questions and other learning features.

Productivity Press Development Team, *Quick Changeover for Operators: The SMED System* (Productivity Press, 1996). This Shopfloor Series book describes the stages of changeover improvement with examples and illustrations.

Productivity Press Development Team, *Mistake-Proofing for Operators: The ZQC System* (Productivity Press, 1997). This Shopfloor Series book describes the basic theory behind mistake-proofing and introduces poka-yoke systems for preventing errors that lead to defects.

Productivity Development Team, *Cellular Manufacturing: One-Piece Flow for Workteams* (Productivity Press, 1999). This Shopfloor Series book introduces basic cellular manufacturing and teamwork concepts to production teams, and orients them for participating in the design of a new production cell.

Productivity Press Development Team, *Kanban for the Shopfloor* (Productivity Press, 2002). This Shopfloor Series book will help your shopfloor workers understand, plan, and implement kanban to reduce overproduction, the most critical of the seven deadly wastes of manufacturing.

Productivity Press Development Team, *Standard Work for the Shopfloor* (Productivity Press, 2002). Adherence to standards protects quality, efficiency, safety, and predictability. This Shopfloor Series book will tell you how to create and communicate standards and standard work. It also provides examples of applications.

Productivity Press Development Team, *Pull Production for the Shopfloor* (Productivity Press, 2002). In this Shopfloor Series book you will learn how the various lean methodologies work together to create a pull system, and how to use production leveling, line balancing, kanban, one-piece flow, and supplier linking to achieve an integrated pull system.

Productivity Press Development Team, *Kaizen for the Shopfloor* (Productivity Press, 2002). This Shopfloor Series book will help everyone in the plant understand the need for daily continuous improvement and will teach, step by step, how to prepare for, implement, and follow up a focused kaizen event.

Productivity Development Team, *OEE for Operators: Overall Equipment Effectiveness* (Productivity Press, 1999). This Shopfloor Series book teaches the critical measurement tools you need to determine how well your equipment is running so that you can take steps to reach and sustain its full potential.

Productivity Development Team, *TPM for Supervisors* (Productivity Press, 1996). This Shopfloor Series book gives frontline supervisors an overview of basic TPM features and implementation and helps them understand their role in making it successful.

Kunio Shirose (ed.), *TPM Team Guide* (Productivity Press, 1995). This Shopfloor Series book emphasizes the integration of TPM with production management and reviews team-based improvement from goal setting to standardization. It discusses problem solving and how to prepare an effective presentation of results.

Japan Institute of Plant Maintenance (ed.), *TPM for Every Operator* (Productivity Press, 1996). This Shopfloor Series book introduces basic concepts of TPM, with emphasis on the six big equipment-related losses, autonomous maintenance activities, and safety.

Japan Institute of Plant Maintenance (ed.), *Autonomous Maintenance for Operators* (Productivity Press, 1997). This Shopfloor Series book on key autonomous maintenance activities includes chapters on cleaning/inspection, lubrication, localized containment of contamination, and one-point lessons related to maintenance.

Japan Institute of Plant Maintenance (ed.), *Focused Equipment Improvement for TPM Teams* (Productivity Press, 1997). This Shopfloor Series book will give your TPM teams a framework for further improving equipment performance by looking at specific losses and design weaknesses that everyone previously thought they had to accept.

Other Books and Videos

Lean Manufacturing Methods

Hiroyuki Hirano, *JIT Implementation Manual: The Complete Guide to Just-in-Time Manufacturing* (Productivity Press, 1990). This two-volume manual is a comprehensive, illustrated guide to every aspect of the lean manufacturing transformation.

Pascal Dennis, *Lean Production Simplified: A Plain Language Guide to the World's Most Powerful Production System* (Productivity Press, 2002). This book is an "on the floor" reference to each component of a lean system. It helps the reader grasp the lean production system as a whole with a plain-language discussion of background, goals, problem solving, and methods that encourage full employee participation.

John W. Davis, *Fast Track to Waste-Free Manufacturing: Straight Talk from a Plant Manager* (Productivity Press, 1999). Using the four drivers of workplace organization, uninterrupted flow, error-free process, and insignificant changeover, this plant manager describes a system to rapidly deploy the lean manufacturing process. He addresses critical issues and provides tools, techniques, checklists, and an ongoing case study to help you move quickly from mass to waste-free manufacturing.

Jeffrey Liker, *Becoming Lean: Inside Stories of U.S. Manufacturers* (Productivity Press, 1997). This book shares powerful first-hand accounts of the complete process of implementing cellular manufacturing, just-in-time, and other aspects of lean production.

Nancy Hyer and Urban Wemmerlov, *Reorganizing the Factory: Competing Through Cellular Manufacturing* (Productivity Press, 2001). This book will give you a "life cycle" approach to the many issues you must address if you are going to get what the authors call *the cell advantage*. You will learn how to justify, design, implement, operate, and improve cells for your environment.

Shigeo Shingo, *A Study of the Toyota Production System: From an Industrial Engineering Viewpoint* (Productivity Press, 1989). This classic book was written by the renowned industrial engineer who helped develop key elements of the Toyota system's success.

Japan Management Association (ed.), *Kanban and Just-in-Time at Toyota: Management Begins at the Workplace* (Productivity Press, 1986). This classic overview describes the underlying concepts and main techniques of the original lean manufacturing system.

Hiroyuki Hirano, *JIT Factory Revolution: A Pictorial Guide to Factory Design of the Future* (Productivity Press, 1988). This book of photographs and diagrams gives an excellent overview of the changes involved in implementing a lean, cellular manufacturing system.

Taiichi Ohno, *Toyota Production System: Beyond Large-Scale Production* (Productivity Press, 1988). This is the story of the first lean manufacturing system, told by the Toyota vice president who was responsible for implementing it.

Iwao Kobayashi, *20 Keys to Workplace Improvement* (Productivity Press, 1995). This book addresses 20 key areas in which a company must improve to maintain a world-class manufacturing operation. A five-step improvement for each key is described and illustrated.

Ken'ichi Sekine, *One-Piece Flow: Cell Design for Transforming the Production Process* (Productivity Press, 1992). This comprehensive book describes how to redesign the factory layout for the most effective deployment of equipment and people; it includes many examples and illustrations.

The 5S System and Visual Management

Tel-A-Train and the Productivity Press Development Team, *The 5S System: Workplace Organization and Standardization* (Tel-A-Train, 1997). Filmed at leading U.S. companies, this seven-tape training package (co-produced with Productivity Press) teaches shopfloor teams how to implement the 5S System.

Michel Greif, *The Visual Factory: Building Participation Through Shared Information* (Productivity Press, 1991). This book shows how visual management techniques can provide just-in-time information to support teamwork and employee participation on the factory floor.

Poka-Yoke (Mistake-Proofing) and Zero Quality Control

C. Martin Hinckley, *Make No Mistake: An Outcome Approach to Mistake-Proofing* (Productivity Press, 2001). In this book you will find many of the best methods for reducing complexity, variation, confusion, and other root causes of defects. And you will learn an outcome-based mistake-proofing classification system that will help you focus on preventing rather than detecting defects.

Shigeo Shingo, *Zero Quality Control: Source Inspection and the Poka-Yoke System* (Productivity Press, 1986). This classic book tells how Shingo developed his ZQC approach. It includes a detailed introduction to poka-yoke devices and many examples of their application in different situations.

NKS/Factory Magazine (ed.), *Poka-Yoke: Improving Product Quality by Preventing Defects* (Productivity Press, 1988). This illustrated book shares 240 poka-yoke examples implemented at different companies to catch errors and prevent defects.

Quick Changeover

Shigeo Shingo, *A Revolution in Manufacturing: The SMED System* (Productivity Press, 1985). This classic book tells the story of Shingo's SMED System, describes how to implement it, and provides many changeover improvement examples.

Facilitation and Tools for Team Empowerment

Walter J. Michalski, *Tool Navigator: Master Guide for Teams* (Productivity Press, 1990). This compendium of over 222 facilitation and problem-solving tools on CD ROM will make it easy for improvement teams to get the most out of their efforts.

Newsletter

Lean Manufacturing Advisor—News and case studies on how companies are implementing lean manufacturing philosophy and specific techniques such as pull production, kanban, cell design, and so on. For subscription information, call 1-800-394-6868.

Training and Consulting

Productivity Consulting Group offers a full range of consulting and training services on lean manufacturing approaches. For additional information, call 1-800-394-6868.

Website

Visit our web pages at www.productivityinc.com to learn more about Productivity's products and services related to identifying and eliminating waste.

About the Productivity Press Development Team

Since 1979, Productivity, Inc. has been publishing and teaching the world's best methods for achieving manufacturing excellence. At the core of this effort is a team of dedicated product developers, including writers, instructional designers, editors, and producers, as well as content experts with years of experience in the field. Hands-on experience and networking keep the team in touch with changes in manufacturing as well as in knowledge sharing and delivery. The team also learns from customers and applies this knowledge to create effective vehicles that serve the learning needs of every level in the organization.

About the Shopfloor Series

Put powerful and proven improvement tools in the hands of your entire workforce!

Progressive shopfloor improvement techniques are imperative for manufacturers who want to stay competitive and to achieve world class excellence. And it's the comprehensive education of all shopfloor workers that ensures full participation and success when implementing new programs. The Shopfloor Series books make practical information accessible to everyone by presenting major concepts and tools in simple, clear language.

Books currently in the Shopfloor Series include:

5S FOR OPERATORS
5 Pillars of the Visual Workplace
The Productivity Press Development Team
ISBN 1-56327-123-0 / 133 pages
Order 5SOP-BK / $25.00

QUICK CHANGEOVER FOR OPERATORS
The SMED System
The Productivity Press Development Team
ISBN 1-56327-125-7 / 93 pages
Order QCOOP-BK / $25.00

MISTAKE-PROOFING FOR OPERATORS
The Productivity Press Development Team
ISBN 1-56327-127-3 / 93 pages
Order ZQCOP-BK / $25.00

JUST-IN-TIME FOR OPERATORS
The Productivity Press Development Team
ISBN 1-56327-134-6 / 96 pages
Order JITOP-BK / $25.00

TPM FOR EVERY OPERATOR
The Japan Institute of Plant Maintenance
ISBN 1-56327-080-3 / 136 pages
Order TPMEO-BK / $25.00

TPM FOR SUPERVISORS
The Productivity Press Development Team
ISBN 1-56327-161-3 / 96 pages
Order TPMSUP-BK / $25.00

TPM TEAM GUIDE
Kunio Shirose
ISBN 1-56327-079-X / 175 pages
Order TGUIDE-BK / $25.00

AUTONOMOUS MAINTENANCE
The Japan Institute of Plant Maintenance
ISBN 1-56327-082-x / 138 pages
Order AUTOMOP-BK / $25.00

FOCUSED EQUIPMENT IMPROVEMENT FOR TPM TEAMS
The Japan Institute of Plant Maintenance
ISBN 1-56327-081-1 / 144 pages
Order FEIOP-BK / $25.00

OEE FOR OPERATORS
The Productivity Press Development Team
ISBN 1-56327-221-0 / 96 pages
Order OEEOP-BK / $25.00

CELLULAR MANUFACTURING
One-Piece Flow for Workteams
The Productivity Press Development Team
ISBN 1-56327-213-X / 96 pages
Order CELL-BK / $25.00

KANBAN FOR THE SHOPFLOOR
The Productivity Press Development Team
ISBN 1-56327-269-5 / 120 pages
Order KANOP-BK / $25.00

KAIZEN FOR THE SHOPFLOOR
The Productivity Press Development Team
ISBN 1-56327-272-5 / 112 pages
Order KAIZOP-BK / $25.00

PULL PRODUCTION FOR THE SHOPFLOOR
The Productivity Press Development Team
ISBN 1-56327-274-1 / 122 pages
Order PULLOP-BK / $25.00

STANDARD WORK FOR THE SHOPFLOOR
The Productivity Press Development Team
ISBN 1-56327-273-3 / 112 pages
Order STANOP-BK / $25.00

IDENTIFYING WASTE ON THE SHOPFLOOR
The Productivity Press Development Team
ISBN 1-56327-287-3 / 112 pages
Order WASTEOP-BK / $25.00

Productivity Press, 444 Park Avenue South, Suite 604, New York, NY 10016
Customer Service Department: Telephone **1-800-394-6868** Fax **1-800-394-6286**